SANITATION WORKER EXAM 2020

NEW YORK CITY

Prepare for Success!

Angelo Tropea

ISBN: 9781698516561

Please note that the passages, examples and questions used in this book are for study purposes only and do **NOT** reflect official names, codes, policy, rules or procedures of any governmental or public or private agency or department.

Unless otherwise clearly indicated, any similarity of names of persons, addresses, places and telephone numbers used in this book to any actual names of persons, addresses and telephone numbers is purely coincidental.

Reader Comments from Prior Edition

"Gets straight to the point to help you pass your test."

"I Just Took The Test and All I Can Say Is This Book Definitely Gets You Prepared. Was Very Helpful, Very. "

"The best of the best. Can't go wrong. This will prepare you like no other. Highly recommended for anyone in the near future. This will definitely prepare you well for the test."

"Excellent book covering all 7 parts of the DSNY Entrance Exam. Each part is broken up in sections so you can practice for the test and get a head start on everyone else."

[1] Notice of Examination Sanitation Worker, 2014
* Wikipedia.org

CONTENTS

SANITATION WORKER 2020
NEW YORK CITY

What the Job Involves

Sanitation Workers, under direct supervision, perform work, and prepare and operate various types of equipment involved in street cleaning, waste collection, recycling collection, snow removal, encumbrance removal, waste disposal; and, when assigned, perform enforcement duties. They follow route sheet of assigned work area; load and unload waste materials and bulk items; monitor collected waste for hazardous or toxic materials; sweep and clean city streets; inspect, prepare, and drive department vehicles and equipment; during winter months, attach and operate snow plows, remove snow and ice from city streets and arterial roadways, and spread salt and sand; use operational manuals and instructional materials; prepare reports, records, and forms; enter data; make log entries; and perform related work.

Special Working Conditions

Sanitation Workers are required to work rotating shifts, rotating days off, nights, Saturdays, Sundays, holidays and mandatory overtime. Additionally, Sanitation Workers are required to perform these tasks in all types of weather.

Some of the physical activities performed by Sanitation Workers and environmental conditions experienced are: walking and/or standing for long periods of time; operating various types of Sanitation Department equipment in all types of weather; pulling, dragging, lifting and carrying heavy and large objects, bags of garbage, cans, containers, bulk items and throwing or dumping them into a truck hopper or loading them onto a truck.

(This is a brief description of what you might do in this position and does not include all the duties of this position.)[1]

SANITATION WORKER   1

INTRODUCTION

You must score well on the New York City Sanitation Worker Exam to be considered for appointment.

Because of this, the aim of this book is to keep it **simple and focused** on the **Sanitation Worker 2020 Written Exam**, instead of complicating it with other information about the job that can be better learned from the New York City web page, "Department of Sanitation New York City."

SIMPLE AND FOCUSED

Relying on printed books or unofficial websites for this type of detailed information is <u>not</u> wise, as the information may be amended by New York City at any time.

To obtain the most complete and up to date information, visit New York City DCAS website and the Department of Sanitation website.

To see the results from the last exam and other sanitation worker information visit:

http://www.nyc.gov/html/dcas/html/work/sanitation_worker_exam_5001_results.shtml

Another valuable resource is the official "<u>NOTICE OF EXAMINATION: SANITATION WORKER</u>" (Also available on the web.)

Please refer to the <u>current official exam announcement</u> for the most up to date information.

Among the topics usually covered on the **Notice of Examination** are the following:

• Exam number	• Required Form (Application for examination)
• When to apply	-----
• Application fee	• The test (general information)
• The test date	-----
-----	• New York City residency credit
• What the job involves	• Admission card
• The salary	-----
• How to apply	• The test results
• How to qualify	-----
• DSNY-provided CDL Training Program	• Additional information
• Driving requirement	Probationary period
• Age requirement	Investigation
• Medical requirement	-----
• Drug screening requirement	• Special test accommodations
• Residency requirement	
• English requirement	
• Proof of identity	

As we said before, our aim is not to repeat what the Department of Sanitation and DCAS already say well at their web site and current exam official announcement, but to provide **EXERCISES, EXPLANATIONS, and HINTS** about the types of questions that may be asked on the written test with the aim of maximizing your score and thereby increasing your chances of getting the job - FAST!

Please note

The New York City Sanitation Worker Exam has been carefully and professionally crafted to separate unprepared candidates and candidates with limited ability and enthusiasm from candidates who have superior ability and who have prepared for the exam.

Although the Sanitation Exam does not test for technical expertise or advanced academic knowledge, it does require serious preparation.

A well thought out plan for tackling the different types of questions is both advisable and important for maximizing your score.

<u>A difference of ONE point may put you ahead of hundreds of other candidates who have taken the exam.</u>

Your decision to study with this book already has set you apart from candidates who will rush into the test unprepared.

Now that you have this book, take advantage of its benefits. Study with it every day from now until the day of the test.

"Always bear in mind that your own resolution to succeed is more important than any other thing."

- Abraham Lincoln

TYPES OF QUESTIONS[1]

Written Comprehension
understanding written sentences and paragraphs. This ability may be used to read and understand departmental messages.

Written Expression
using English words or sentences in writing so that others will understand. This ability may be used to complete a form for a specific request such as switching a vacation day.

Problem Sensitivity
being able to tell when something is wrong or is likely to go wrong. It includes being able to identify the whole problem as well as elements of the problem. This ability may be used to tell if there is something wrong with the waste collection truck, which will lead to a mechanical failure.

Information Ordering
following correctly a rule or set of rules or actions in a certain order. The rule or set of rules used are given. The things or actions to be put in order can include numbers, letters, words, pictures, procedures, sentences, and mathematical or logical operations. This ability may be used to understand the correct order in which a plow must be assembled.

Deductive Reasoning
applying general rules to specific problems and coming up with logical answers. It involves deciding if an answer makes sense. This ability may be used to determine which type of waste to collect, based on specific waste collection rules.

Spatial Orientation
determining where you are in relation to the location of some object or where the object is in relation to you. For example, this ability may be used to determine where to drive to reach a destination located a few blocks away.

Visualization
imagining how something would look when it is moved around or when its parts are moved or rearranged. It requires the forming of mental images of how patterns or objects would look after certain changes, such as unfolding or rotation. One has to predict how an object, set of objects, or pattern will appear after the changes have been carried out. This ability may be used to assemble a plow based on an illustration.

WRITTEN COMPREHENSION 2

Written Comprehension

A written passage is presented and questions are asked that require you to carefully refer back to the passage.

These questions may be designed to evaluate your ability to understand the conclusions in the passage or in noticing specific details that are presented.

Suggestions

Read the passage carefully. Try to understand what the main subject is and what conclusions, if any, are being expressed.

Look at the question relating to the paragraph. Is the answer clear and obvious? If not, read the passage again with the aim of finding the specific section that provides the correct answer.

Pay attention to the details of the four answer choices A, B, C, & D.

The correct answer choice will be the choice that matches all the details.

To double-check your answer, look at all the choices that you considered incorrect and try to find a specific reason why each of them is not the correct answer.

Why are written comprehension questions asked?

The responsibilities of Sanitation Workers include the use of operational manuals and instructional materials, the preparation of reports, records and forms, the entering of data and the making of log entries. The ability of a Sanitation Worker to read and understand written material is therefore very important. The reading comprehension questions of the test measure how well you read and understand written material.

Reading Comprehension Questions Format:

1. A brief reading selection (one or more paragraphs) may be provided.
2. After the paragraph there are one or more multiple choice questions for you to answer.
3. After carefully reading the paragraph, you must answer the questions **based ONLY on the information contained in the paragraph**.

The following are some examples of Written Comprehension Questions:

Example 1 Question:

In the NYC Sanitation Department all overtime policy must be uniform and applied fairly in all cases. First, the decision to work overtime is not at the discretion of Sanitation Workers. It may be mandated when necessary if other suitable volunteer employees are not available to perform the work during the overtime period. Although certain duties may be performed by all employees in any NYC Sanitation job title, some duties must be performed only by employees in designated job titles or who have successfully completed required training. An example of this may be found in the preparation of NYC Central Collection Reports. These reports may only be prepared by Sanitation Workers who have more than five years of experience as a Sanitation Worker and who have completed the required statistical training course.

1. Which of the following statements is supported by the preceding paragraph?

A. All employees may prepare NYC Central Collection Reports.

B. All employees must prepare NYC Central Collection Reports.

C. NYC Central Collection Reports may be prepared by all employees who have completed the required statistical training course.

D. none of the above

Example 1 Answer:

In the NYC Sanitation Department all overtime policy must be uniform and applied fairly in all cases. First, the decision to work overtime is not at the discretion of Sanitation Workers. It may be mandated when necessary if other suitable volunteer employees are not available to perform the work during the overtime period. Although certain duties may be performed by all employees in any NYC Sanitation job title, **some duties must be performed only by employees in designated job titles or who have successfully completed required training**. An example of this may be found in the preparation of NYC Central Collection Reports. These reports may only be prepared by Sanitation Workers who have more than five years of experience as a Sanitation Worker **and** who have completed the required statistical training course.

1. Which of the following statements is <u>supported</u> by the preceding paragraph?

A. All employees may prepare NYC Central Collection Reports.

B. All employees must prepare NYC Central Collection Reports.

C. NYC Central Collection Reports may be prepared by all employees who have completed the required statistical training course.

D. **None of the above**

The correct answer is "D. None of the above."

"A" is not a correct statement because NYC Central Collection Reports may be prepared <u>only</u> by employees who have completed the required statistical training course <u>and</u> who have five years of experience.

"B" is not a correct statement because only employees who are qualified may prepare the statistical reports.

"C" is not a correct statement because in addition to completing the required statistical training course, Sanitation Workers must <u>also</u> have five years of experience.

"D" is the answer **because it correctly states that "A", "B," and "C" are not supported by the passage.**

Example 2 Question:

Sanitation workers have a number of promotional opportunities. One of these is promotion to "Supervisor (Sanitation)." According to Exam No. 4509 Amended Notice: January 29, 2014, "...to be eligible for promotion, you must have completed your probationary period in the eligible title as indicated in the above "Eligibility To Take Examination" section, and have served permanently as a Sanitation Worker for two (2) years. Additionally, you must be permanently employed in the eligible title or your name must appear on a Preferred List for the eligible title at the time of promotion."

2. According to the preceding passage, which of the following statements is not correct?

A. A person on probation in the specified "eligible title" cannot be appointed a "Supervisor (Sanitation)."

B. At the time of promotion to "Supervisor (Sanitation)," you must have served in a temporary title for at least two years.

C. The Promotion to "Supervisor (Sanitation) Exam No. 4509 Amended Notice" is dated January 29, 2014.

D. At the time of appointment, one of the requirements to be promoted to "Supervisor (Sanitation)," is that you must be permanently employed in the eligible title or your name must appear on a Preferred List for the eligible title.

Example 2 Answer:

Sanitation workers have a number of promotional opportunities. One of these is promotion to "Supervisor (Sanitation)." According to Exam No. 4509 Amended Notice: January 29, 2014, "...to be eligible for promotion, <u>you must have completed your probationary period in the eligible title as indicated in the above "Eligibility To Take Examination" section, and have served **permanently** as a Sanitation Worker for two (2) years</u>. Additionally, you must be permanently employed in the eligible title or your name must appear on a Preferred List for the eligible title at the time of promotion."

2. According to the preceding passage, which of the following statements is <u>not</u> correct?

A. A person on probation in the specified "eligible title" cannot be appointed a "Supervisor (Sanitation)." (This is a correct statement and therefore it is not the answer: "...,you must have <u>completed</u> your probationary period in the eligible title....")

B. <u>At the time of promotion to "Supervisor (Sanitation)," you must have served in a temporary title for at least two years</u>. **(This statement is NOT CORRECT, therefore "B" is the answer.** "...you must have completed your probationary period in the eligible title as indicated in the above "Eligibility To Take Examination" section, <u>and</u> have served <u>permanently</u> as a Sanitation Worker for two (2) years.")

C. The Promotion to "Supervisor (Sanitation)" Exam No. 4509 Amended Notice is dated January 29, 2014. (This is a correct statement and therefore it is not the answer.)

D. At the time of appointment, one of the requirements to be promoted to "Supervisor (Sanitation)," is that you must be permanently employed in the eligible title or your name must appear on a Preferred List for the eligible title." (This is a correct statement and therefore it is not the answer.)

Example 3 Question:

Properly preparing reports is an important part of a Sanitation Worker's duties. This is especially true when filling out incident reports for "aided" cases or "unusual occurrences." An "Aided" report is used when a Sanitation Worker assists a New York City employee or a member of the public who has been injured and requires emergency or medical assistance. "Unusual Occurrence" reports are prepared for other types of incidents, including discovery of weapons or illegal substances. In addition to providing a paper trail for legal and liability reasons, these reports are a valuable resource when reviewing staffing, procedures, work performance, and planning.

3. According to the above selection:

A. An "Aided" incident report is used to document the discovery of a pouch containing heroin.

B. "Aided" and "Unusual Occurrence" reports prevent lawsuits against Sanitation Workers.

C. An "Aided" report is filled out if a Sanitation Worker calls for an ambulance for an injured person.

D. An "Aided" report must be filled out if waste is collected from a residence where a person with disabilities resides.

Example 3 Answer:

Properly preparing reports is an important part of a Sanitation Worker's duties. This is especially true when filling out incident reports for "aided" cases or "unusual occurrences." An **"Aided" report is used when a Sanitation Worker assists a New York City employee or a member of the public who was been injured and requires emergency or medical assistance**. "Unusual Occurrence" reports are prepared for other types of incidents, including discovery of weapons or illegal substances. In addition to providing a paper trail for legal and liability reasons, these reports are a valuable resource when reviewing staffing, procedures, work performance, and planning.

3. According to the above selection:

A. An "Aided" incident report is used to document the discovery of a pouch containing heroin. (This statement is <u>not</u> correct and therefore it is not the answer. "An Aided report is used when a Sanitation Worker assists a New York City employee or a member of the public who was been injured and requires <u>emergency or medical assistance</u>. ")

B. "Aided" and "Unusual Occurrence" reports prevent lawsuits against Sanitation Workers. (This statement is <u>not</u> correct and therefore it is not the answer. "In addition to <u>providing a paper trail</u> for legal and liability reasons, these reports are a valuable resource when reviewing staffing, procedures, work performance, and planning." These reports provide a paper trail, but do not prevent lawsuits.)

C. **An "Aided" report is filled out if a Sanitation Worker calls for an ambulance for an injured person. (THIS IS THE ANSWER because it is a correct statement.** The passage states, "An "Aided" report is used when a Sanitation Worker assists a New York City employee or a member of the public who has <u>been injured and requires emergency or medical assistance</u>.")

D. An "Aided" report must be filled out if waste is collected from a residence where a person with disabilities resides. (This statement is <u>not</u> correct and therefore it is not the answer. (The Aided Report is used when the Sanitation Worker provides emergency or <u>medical assistance</u>.)

Example 4 Question:

A famous person once said that in discussions among persons, what often has the greatest impact is what is left unsaid. A polite reminder and a firm and balanced glance from a Sanitation Worker sometimes has more effect than a loud rebuke concerning improper recycle separation. The "glance" or "look," however, has little effect when not supported by a professional and determined appearance. Sanitation Workers should therefore be well groomed and always be in clean and appropriate uniform.

4. According to the above passage, which of the following statements is correct?

A. Sanitation Workers should never speak loudly.

B. Sanitation Workers should always wear all the parts of their uniform.

C. Sanitation Workers should not look at persons if they are not in appropriate uniform.

D. Appearance is important in performing some of the duties of a Sanitation Worker.

Example 4 Answer:

A famous person once said that in discussions among persons, what often has the greatest impact is what is left unsaid. A polite reminder and a firm and balanced glance from a Sanitation Worker sometimes has more effect than a loud rebuke concerning improper recycle separation. The "glance" or "look," however, has little effect when not supported by a <u>professional and determined appearance. Sanitation Workers should therefore be well groomed and always be in clean and appropriate uniform.</u>

4. According to the above passage, which of the following statements is <u>correct</u>?

A. Sanitation Workers should never speak loudly.

   (This statement is <u>not</u> correct and therefore it is not the answer. The passage deals with not speaking loudly <u>at the time of informing the public regarding recycle rules</u> and NOT at any other time, including an emergency when a loud alert may be required to avoid injury.)

B. Sanitation Workers should always wear all the parts of their uniform. (This statement is <u>not</u> correct and therefore it is not the answer. The passage states, "Sanitation Workers should therefore be well groomed and always be in clean and <u>appropriate</u> uniform." The uniform of a Sanitation Worker differs according to the season. Sanitation Workers are not required to wear their winter garments in summer.)

C. Sanitation Workers should not look at persons if they are not in appropriate uniform.

   (This statement is <u>not</u> correct and therefore it is not the answer. The passage deals with the way Sanitation Workers look at persons at the time of informing the public regarding recycle procedure and also recommends proper "glances" or "looks" at other times, but it does not recommend that Sanitation Workers not look at people when they are not in appropriate uniform.)

D. <u>**Appearance is important when performing some of the duties of a Sanitation Worker**</u>. **(This statement is correct and therefore "D" is the answer.** The main emphasis of the passage is the importance of a "professional and determined appearance.")

Example 5 Question:

One of the greatest challenges that a Sanitation Worker faces is the application of broad policies and procedures to specific situations. Unlike specific guidelines, broad policies prescribe the boundaries of acceptable behaviors and responses to a wide spectrum of applications. Thus, for example, there is a firm Sanitation Department policy that Sanitation Workers do not collect business waste, without there also being specific prescribed answers to the myriad questions that may arise under different situations.

5. According to the preceding passage:

A. Specific procedures are preferable to broad procedures.

B. Broad procedures are preferable to specific outlines.

C. Sanitation Workers must apply Sanitation Department policies to specific situations.

D. The Sanitation Department should provide specific policies and procedures for all situations that may arise.

Example 5 Answer:

<u>One of the greatest challenges that a Sanitation Worker faces is the application of broad policies and procedures to specific situations.</u> Unlike specific guidelines, broad policies prescribe the boundaries of acceptable behaviors and responses to a wide spectrum of applications. Thus, for example, there is a firm Sanitation Department policy that Sanitation Workers do not collect business waste, without there also being specific prescribed answers to the myriad questions that may arise under different situations.

5. According to the preceding passage:

A. Specific procedures are preferable to broad procedures. (This statement is <u>not</u> correct and therefore choice "A" is not the answer. The passage deals with applying broad policies and procedures to specific situations and <u>not</u> the preferability of specific procedures over broad policies.)

B. Broad procedures are preferable to specific outlines. (This statement is <u>not</u> correct and therefore this choice is not the answer. The passage deals with applying broad policies and procedures to specific situations and <u>not</u> the preferability of broad procedures over specific outlines.)

C. **<u>Sanitation Workers must apply Sanitation Department policies to specific situations</u>. (This statement is correct and therefore choice "C" is the answer.** The entire passage deals with the importance of applying broad policies to specific situations.)

D. The Sanitation Department should provide specific policies and procedures for all situations that may arise. (This statement is <u>not</u> correct and therefore this choice is not the answer. The passage does <u>not</u> recommend the issuance of specific policies and procedures for all situations that may arise.)

Example 6 Question:

Smoking in NYC Sanitation District Offices is not permitted, except in designated areas. A member of the public who is found to be smoking in an area where smoking is not permitted must be asked by the Sanitation Officer to extinguish what he is smoking. If the person refuses to do so, the Sanitation Officer shall ask the person to remove himself from the facility and if the person refuses, the Sanitation Officer may charge the person with the appropriate violation of law. An employee found to be smoking in an area where smoking is not permitted must be asked by the Sanitation Officer to extinguish what the employee is smoking, and if the employee refuses, the Sanitation Officer must file an Unusual Incident Report which will subject the employee to disciplinary charges.

6. According to the preceding passage:

A. An incident report must be filled out if a member of the public is found smoking in a NYC Sanitation District Office.

B. An employee who smokes in an area where smoking is not permitted must be charged with the appropriate violation of law.

C. Smoking is not permitted in fifty per cent of NYC Sanitation District Offices.

D. An Unusual Incident Report must be filled out if an employee who is smoking in an area where smoking is not permitted does not comply with a request by a Sanitation Officer to stop smoking.

Example 6 Answer:

Smoking in NYC Sanitation District Offices is not permitted, except in designated areas. A member of the public who is found to be smoking in an area where smoking is not permitted must be asked by the Sanitation Officer to extinguish what he is smoking. If the person refuses to do so, the Sanitation Officer shall ask the person to remove himself from the facility and if the person refuses, the Sanitation Officer may charge the person with the appropriate violation of law. An **employee** found to be smoking in an area where smoking is not permitted must be asked by the Sanitation Officer to extinguish what the employee is smoking, and if the employee refuses, **the Sanitation Officer must file an Unusual Incident Report which will subject the employee to disciplinary charges**.

6. According to the preceding passage:

A. An incident report must be filled out if a member of the public is found smoking in a NYC Sanitation District Office. (This statemen is <u>not</u> correct and therefore this choice is not the answer. "...if the <u>employee</u> refuses, the Sanitation Officer must fill out an unusual incident report.")

B. An employee who smokes in an area where smoking is not permitted must be charged with the appropriate violation of law. (This statement is not correct and therefore this is not the answer choice. "An employee found to be smoking in an area where smoking is not permitted must be asked by the Sanitation Officer to extinguish what the employee is smoking, and if the employee refuses, the Sanitation Officer must fill out an unusual incident report which will subject the employee to disciplinary charges.")

C. Smoking is not permitted in fifty per cent of NYC Sanitation District Offices. (This is <u>not</u> correct and therefore this is not the answer choice. This passage does not deal at all with the <u>percentage</u> of NYC Sanitation District Offices where smoking in not permitted.)

D. **An Unusual Incident Report must be filled out if an employee who is smoking in an area where smoking is not permitted resists a request by a Sanitation Officer to stop smoking**. (THIS IS THE CORRECT ANSWER. "An employee found to be smoking in an area where smoking is not permitted must be asked by the Sanitation Officer to extinguish what the employee is smoking, and if the employee refuses, the Sanitation Officer must file an unusual incident report which will subject the employee to disciplinary charges.")

Example 7 Question:

The Americans With Disabilities Act applies to all public buildings, whether they are city or state owned or owned by private entities. It requires New York City to make reasonable accommodations for people with disabilities. In structures completed before January 1, 1994, reasonable accommodations may be made by physical modification of existing structures to meet ADA guidelines or by establishing procedures to otherwise reasonably accommodate people with disabilities. For example, in structures built after January 1, 1994, an entrance ramp must be provided where the first floor entrance is above street level. In structures built before January 1, 1994 an alternative entrance, such as a back entrance, may be used if it provides access to the building at ground level.*

7. According to the above paragraph:

A. All back entrances to buildings must be at ground level.

B. An entrance ramp must be provided in all court buildings built after January 1, 1994.

C. ADA requirements require physical modification of existing structures.

D. ADA rules apply to all public buildings.

Example 7 Answer:

The Americans With Disabilities Act applies to all public buildings, whether they are city or state owned or owned by private entities. It requires the New York City to make reasonable accommodations for people with disabilities. In structures completed before January 1, 1994, reasonable accommodations may be made by physical modification of existing structures to meet ADA guidelines or by establishing procedures to otherwise reasonably accommodate people with disabilities. For example, in structures built after January 1, 1994, an entrance ramp must be provided where the first floor entrance is above street level. In structures built before January 1, 1994 an <u>alternative</u> entrance, such as a back entrance, may be used if it provides access to the building at ground level.*

7. According to the above paragraph:

A. All back entrances to buildings must be at ground level. (This statement is <u>not</u> correct and therefore this is not the answer choice. "In structures built before January 1, 1994 an <u>alternative entrance</u>, such as a back entrance, **may** be used if it provides access to the building at ground level.")

B. An entrance ramp must be provided in all court buildings built after January 1, 1994. (This statement is not correct and therefore this is not the answer choice. "For example, in structures built after January 1, 1994, an entrance ramp must be provided **where the first floor entrance is above street level**.")

C. All ADA requirements require physical modification of existing structures. (This statement is <u>not</u> correct and therefore this is not the answer choice. "In structures completed before January 1, 1994, reasonable accommodations may be made by physical modification of existing structures to meet ADA guidelines <u>or</u> by establishing procedures to otherwise reasonably accommodate people with disabilities.**")

D. <u>ADA rules apply to all public buildings.</u>
(THIS IS THE CORRECT ANSWER. "The Americans With Disabilities Act applies to all public buildings.**")**

Example 8 Question:

Although almost all city buildings are air conditioned, in some buildings there are some rooms or areas where the air conditioning system might not always be sufficient. This situation can occur because the power of the air conditioning system might not be adequate for the area, or because the system might be in need of repair. If the temperature in a room rises above 84 degrees, then the employees must be relocated to another room. If there are no areas in the building where the temperature is below 84 degrees, then the employees shall be released with pay for the day. The release of the employees and the resulting suspension of activity in the building must be approved by the head of Facilities, Benjamin Brinks. In his absence, Lance Jefferson of personnel relations may provide the same approval.

8. According to the above, which of the following statements is not correct?

A. Employees working in a room must be relocated if the temperature rises above 84 degrees in the room.

B. If the temperature rises above 84 degrees in all the rooms of a building, only Lance Jefferson may approve the release of employees and suspension of activity.

C. If employees are relocated to a different room, the temperature in the room to which they are relocated may not be more than 82 degrees.

D. Employees properly released due to excessive temperature do not lose any pay due to the release.

Example 8 Answer:

Although almost all city buildings are air conditioned, in some buildings there are some rooms or areas where the air conditioning system might not always be sufficient. This situation can occur because the power of the air conditioning system might not be adequate for the area, or because the system might be in need of repair. If the temperature in a room rises above 84 degrees, then the employees must be relocated to another room. If there are no areas in the building where the temperature is below 84 degrees, then the employees shall be released with pay for the day. **The release of the employees and the resulting suspension of activity in the building must be approved by the head of Facilities, Benjamin Brinks. In his absence, Lance Jefferson of personnel relations may provide the same approval**.

8. According to the above, which of the following statements is <u>not</u> correct?

A. Employees working in a room must be relocated if the temperature rises above 84 degrees in the room. (This statement is correct and therefore it is not the answer. "If the temperature in a room rises above 84 degrees, then the employees must be relocated to another room.")

B. **<u>If the temperature rises above 84 degrees in all the rooms of a city building, only Lance Jefferson may approve the release of employees and suspension of activity</u>. (This is the ANSWER because this statement is <u>not</u> correct.** "The release of the employees and the resulting suspension of activity in the building must be prior approved by the head of Facilities, Benjamin Brinks. <u>In his absence</u>, Lance Jefferson of personnel relations may provide the same approval.")

C. If employees are relocated to a different room, the temperature in the room to which they are relocated may not be more than 84 degrees. (This statement is correct and therefore it is not the answer. "If the temperature in a room rises above 84 degrees, then the employees must be relocated to another room.")

D. Employees properly released due to excessive temperature do not lose any pay due to the release. (This statement is correct and therefore it is not the answer. "If there are no areas in the building where the temperature is below 84 degrees, then the employees shall be released <u>with pay</u> for the day.")

WRITTEN EXPRESSION 3

Written Expression

These questions evaluate your ability to express yourself clearly enough so that others will understand.

In one type of written expression question, you may be presented with two or more versions of a written sample.

You are asked to decide which version(s) are clear, accurate, complete, and grammatically correct.

_____

In deciding which sentences are correct, consider the following (one at a time):

Is the **grammar correct**?

Is the **passage clear**?

Is the **information accurate**?

Is the **information complete**?

Written Expression Example

A Sanitation Worker is reviewing a report she is preparing. It contains the following two rough drafts. Which of the two sentences are grammatically correct?

1. Proper training and attitude proper grooming and proper wearing a well maintained uniform are important in conveying a confident and professional appearance

2. In addition to proper training and attitude, proper grooming and the wearing of a well maintained uniform are important in conveying a confident and professional appearance.

A. Only sentence 1 is grammatically correct.
B. Only sentence 2 is grammatically correct.
C. Both sentence 1 and sentence 2 are grammatically correct.
D. Neither sentence 1 nor sentence 2 is grammatically correct.

BEFORE WE ATTEMPT TO ANSWER THE QUESTION, LET'S DEVELOP AN APPROACH TO THIS TYPE OF QUESTION AND ALSO DO A QUICK REVIEW OF SOME RULES OF GRAMMAR, USAGE, PUNCTUATION AND SENTENCE STRUCTURE.

FIRST, READ EACH SENTENCE CAREFULLY AND SEE IF IT HAS ANY OF THE FOLLOWING OBVIOUS FLAWS:

1. DOES IT SOUND LIKE ENGLISH - OR DOES IT SOUND LIKE STREET TALK?
Some obvious examples: (Underlining is for emphasis of correct/incorrect English usage.)
> **Correct:** I <u>go</u> to the store every day.
> **Not Correct:** I <u>goes</u> to the store every day.

> **Correct:** It <u>doesn't</u> matter how much it costs.
> **Not Correct:** It <u>don't</u> matter how much it costs.

2. IS THE SENTENCE IN A LOGICAL SEQUENCE AND MAIN IDEAS PROPERLY CONNECTED?
Example: Which of the following three choices is/are correct?
> 1. The boy who dropped out of high school didn't like to study.
> 2. The boy didn't like to study dropped out of high school.
> 3. The boy dropped out didn't like to study.

Answer: (1) is the most logical, clear, and grammatically correct choice.

3. ARE THERE ANY MISSPELLED WORDS?
Example:
> assistant and NOT asistant
> sanitation facility and NOT sanitation fasility
> believe and NOT beleive
> precinct and NOT precint

4. ARE WORDS USED CORRECTLY?

The principal (NOT principle) of the school was Mr. Kane.
The advice (NOT advise) was very welcomed.
They complimented (NOT complemented) her for her hard work.
Their (NOT there) car needed repair.
He picked up the stationery (NOT stationary) for the supervisor in room 605.
He was too (NOT "to" or "two") happy to speak.
The Sanitation Worker accepted (NOT excepted) the medal.
The work site (NOT cite) was very clean.
Someone who is not moving is stationary. (NOT stationery)
The capital city (NOT capitol) of New York State is Albany.

5. ARE APOSTROPHES USED CORRECTLY?

The boy's (NOT boys) hat was yellow.
The chairs' (NOT chairs, NOT chair's) weave pattern was different on all of them.

IF YOU CANNOT ELIMINATE THE SENTENCE AS BEING BAD BY APPLYING THE ABOVE GENERAL RULES, REVIEW THE SENTENCE FOR THE FOLLOWING GRAMMATICAL FLAWS. (REMEMBER THAT FOR ALL OF THE FOLLOWING RULES, THERE ARE EXCEPTIONS.)

FOR A SENTENCE TO BE COMPLETE, IT MUST HAVE AT MINIMUM A SUBJECT (Who or what the sentence is about) AND A PREDICATE (an action word). OTHERWISE, IT IS JUST A SENTENCE FRAGMENT.

A **subject** is usually a noun about which something is asked or stated.
Example: The Sanitation Worker (subject) speaks softly.

A **predicate** is usually a verb and is the part of the sentence comprising what is said about the subject.
In the above example, the predicate is "speaks."

Usually the subject and the predicate by themselves make up a complete sentence.

	Subject	Predicate
Example	The Sanitation Worker	speaks.

Example of a sentence fragment:
The Sanitation Worker at the counter.
This is a sentence fragment because there is a subject (Sanitation Worker) but no predicate.

Example of a complete sentence:
The **Sanitation Worker** at the counter **speaks** Spanish.
| subject | | predicate |

A VERB AND ITS SUBJECT MUST AGREE IN NUMBER. (singular or plural)
The Sanitation Workers looks tall. (NOT CORRECT)
The Sanitation Workers look tall. (CORRECT)
Sanitation Workers is plural (more than one). "Sanitation Workers" and "look" agree in
__ber.

Another example:

The men and the woman <u>works</u> in the same office. (NOT CORRECT)

The men and the woman <u>work</u> in the same office. (CORRECT)

The men and woman is a plural subject and takes a plural verb <u>work</u>.

The boy <u>works</u> (singular verb). The boy and girl <u>work</u> (plural verb).

A COMMA USUALLY GOES BEFORE THE FOLLOWING WORDS - but, for, or, nor, so, yet - WHEN THE WORD CONNECTS TWO MAIN CLAUSES.

Examples:

He didn't like to study, but he liked to play.

He scored a high mark, for he had received good training.

You can try hard and succeed, or you can make a feeble attempt and fail.

He didn't try hard, nor did he try for long.

He studied long and hard, so he passed.

He was sick when he took the test, yet he did scored high.

A COMMA USUALLY GOES AFTER AN INTRODUCTORY PHRASE.

Examples:

When you study, you build up the neural connections in your brain.

Because of hard work and a little good luck, he succeeded in life.

A COMMA USUALLY GOES BETWEEN SEPARATE ITEMS IN A LIST OR SERIES OF ADJECTIVES.

Examples:

The boy was young, proud, and happy.

The tall, young, proud boy walked up to the front of the room.

COMMAS USUALLY SET OFF PARENTHETICAL ELEMENTS

Examples:

Young boys, <u>as Abraham Lincoln once observed</u>, should not be afraid to work hard.

American soldiers, <u>generally speaking,</u> are very well trained.

A SEMICOLON IS USUALLY USED BETWEEN MAIN CLAUSES NOT LINKED BY and, but, for, or, nor, so, yet.

Examples:

The young boys played basketball; the older men sat on the bleachers.

The war had many battles; few were as fierce as this one.

Notice that the letter after the semicolon is NOT capitalized.

THE COLON IS USUALLY USED TO DIRECT ATTENTION TO A SERIES.

Example:

The ingredients of success are as follows: hard work, commitment, and luck.

Written Expression Questions 1 - 3

1. A Sanitation Worker is reviewing a report she is preparing. It contains the following two rough drafts. Which of the two sentences are grammatically correct?

   1. Proper training and attitude proper grooming and proper wearing of a well maintained uniform are important in conveying a confident and professional appearance

   2. In addition to proper training and attitude, proper grooming and the wearing of a well maintained uniform are important in conveying a confident and professional appearance.

A. Only sentence 1 is grammatically correct.
B. Only sentence 2 is grammatically correct.
C. Both sentence 1 and sentence 2 are grammatically correct.
D. Neither sentence 1 nor sentence 2 is grammatically correct.

----

2. A Sanitation Worker is asked by his partner to review a report that he is preparing. It contains the following two versions of one part of the report. Which are grammatically correct?

   1. Mr Jones stated that although he would accept the open container citation, he would not pay it on principal and that he would immediately tear it up.

   2. Mr Jones said that he would accept the open container citation, but on principle he would not pay it and would immediately tear it up.

A. Only sentence 1 is grammatically correct.
B. Only sentence 2 is grammatically correct.
C. Both sentence 1 and sentence 2 are grammatically correct.
D. Neither sentence 1 nor sentence 2 is grammatically correct.

----

3. A Sanitation Worker is preparing a report and has not decided which of two versions of a specific section he wishes to use. Which of the two versions are grammatically correct?

   1. Mr. Kim Jones and Mr. David Alsbury has not decided whether to testify at the Environmental Control Board hearing. Both believe that the complaint is not merited.

   2. Mr. Kim Jones and Mr. David Alsbury have not decided whether to testify at the Environmental Control hearing. Both beleive that the complaint is not merited.

A. Only sentence 1 is grammatically correct.
B. Only sentence 2 is grammatically correct.
C. Both sentence 1 and sentence 2 are grammatically correct.
D. Neither sentence 1 nor sentence 2 is grammatically correct.

Written Expression Answers 1 – 3

1. A Sanitation Worker is reviewing a report she is preparing. It contains the following two rough drafts. Which of the two sentences are grammatically correct?

1. Proper training and attitude proper grooming and proper wearing of a well maintained uniform are important in conveying a confident and professional appearance

2. In addition to proper training and attitude, proper grooming and the wearing of a well maintained uniform are important in conveying a confident and professional appearance.

B. Only sentence 2 is grammatically correct. (Sentence 1 needs a comma after "attitude" and a period at the end of the sentence.)

----

2. A Sanitation Worker is asked by his partner to review a report that he is preparing. It contains the following two versions of one part of the report. Which are grammatically correct?

1. Mr Jones stated that although he would accept the open container citation, he would not pay it on principal and that he would immediately tear it up.

2. Mr Jones said that he would accept the open container citation, but on principle he would not pay it and would immediately tear it up.

D. Neither sentence 1 nor sentence 2 is grammatically correct. (Both need a period at the end of "Mr." Also, "principal" in sentence 1 should be "principle."

----

3. A Sanitation Worker is preparing a report and has not decided which of two versions of a specific section he wishes to use. Which of the two versions are grammatically correct?

1. Mr. Kim Jones and Mr. David Alsbury has not decided whether to testify at the Environmental Control Board hearing. Both believe that the complaint is not merited.

2. Mr. Kim Jones and Mr. David Alsbury have not decided whether to testify at the Environmental Control Board hearing. Both beleive that the complaint is not merited.

D. Neither sentence 1 nor sentence 2 are grammatically correct. (The "has" in sentence 1 should be "have" and "beleive" in sentence two should be "believe."

Written Expression Questions 4 - 6

4. A Sanitation Worker has volunteered to give a speech at a Community Board meeting. Which of the following two versions are correct?

    1. Persons should call 911 to report emergencies they will receive a fast response.

    2. Persons should call 911 to report emergencies. They will receive a fast response.

A. 1 only is correct.
B. 2 only is correct.
C. Neither 1 nor 2 is correct.
D. Both 1 and 2 are correct.

----

5. A Sanitation Worker is preparing an instruction sheet on how to process reports. Which of the following two versions are correct?

    1. Properly preparing reports is an important part of a Sanitation Workers job. This is especially true when filling out reports of aided cases or unusual occurrences.

    2. Properly preparing reports is an important part of a Sanitation Worker's job this is especially true when filling out reports of aided cases or unusual occurrences.

A. 1 only is correct.
B. 2 only is correct.
C. Neither 1 nor 2 is correct.
D. Both 1 and 2 are correct.

----

6. Sanitation Worker Jane Halsey is checking the correctness of sentences in one of her reports. Which of the following two sentences are correct?

    1. Because rules and reggulations must be clearly understood and correctly applied, your ability to understand and apply facts and information to given situations is vital for the proper performance of your duties.

    2. Because rules and regulations must be clearly understood and correctly applied, your ability to understand and apply facts and information to given situations is vital for the proper performance of your duties.

A. 1 only is correct.   C. Neither 1 nor 2 is correct.
B. 2 only is correct.   D. Both 1 and 2 are correct.

Written Expression Answers 4 – 6

4. A Sanitation Worker has volunteered to give a speech at a Community Board meeting. Which of the following two versions are correct?

    1. Persons should call 911 to report emergencies they will receive a fast response.

    2. Persons should call 911 to report emergencies. They will receive a fast response.

B. 2 only is correct. (Sentence one is a run-on sentence. It needs a period after the word "emergencies" and a capital "T" for the word "they."

----

5. A Sanitation Worker is preparing an instruction sheet on how to process reports. Which of the following two versions are correct?

    1. Properly preparing reports is an important part of a Sanitation Workers job. This is especially true when filling out reports of aided cases or unusual occurrences.

    2. Properly preparing reports is an important part of a Sanitation Worker's job this is especially true when filling out reports of aided cases or unusual occurrences.

A. 1 only is correct.
B. 2 only is correct.
C. Neither 1 nor 2 is correct.
D. Both 1 and 2 are correct.

C. Neither 1 nor 2 is correct. (One is not correct because "a Sanitation Workers" should be " a Sanitation Worker's" – singular possessive. Two is not correct because it is a run-on sentence. It should have a period after "job" and a capital "T" for the word "this."

----

6. Sanitation Worker Jane Halsey is checking the correctness of sentences in one of her reports. Which of the following two sentences are correct?

    1. Because rules and reggulations must be clearly understood and correctly applied, your ability to understand and apply facts and information to given situations is vital for the proper performance of your duties.

2. Because rules and regulations must be clearly understood and correctly applied, your ability to understand and apply facts and information to given situations is vital for the proper performance of your duties.

C. Neither 1 nor 2 is correct. (One is not correct because the word "regulations" is misspelled "reggulations." Two is not correct because the word "performance" is misspelled "performence.")

Another type of **WRITTEN EXPRESSION** question may ask you to select the best summary of information that is provided. (The best summary is the one that expresses the information in the most <u>clear, accurate and complete manner.</u>)

Before we try to answer a question of this type, let's consider the following simple example:

Information provided:

A 16 year old boy was struck by a 2002 Buick on August 17, 2019.

Not clear:

2002 Buick on August 17, 2019, a 16 year old boy. (Connection between details is not clear.)

Clear:

A 2002 Buick, on August 17, 2019, struck a 16 year old boy.

Not accurate:

A 16 year old boy was struck by a 2012 Buick on August 17, 2019. (Year of vehicle is not correct.)

Accurate:

A 16 year old boy was struck by a <u>2002</u> Buick on August 17, 2019.

Not complete:

A boy was struck by a 2002 Buick on August 17, 2019. (Age of boy is missing)

Complete:

A <u>16</u> year old boy was struck by a 2002 Buick on August 17, 2019.

Written Expression Question 7

Sanitation Worker Able is asked to select the best summary (A, B, C or D) of the following information: (The best summary is the one that expresses the information in the **most clear, accurate and complete manner**).

Place of accident: in front of 1726 West 8ᵗʰ Street, Brooklyn

Time of accident: 12:25 P.M.

Date of accident: September 11, 2019

Vehicle involved: waste collection truck No. 284673NYC

Sanitation Worker Driver: Charles Broom

Damage: cracked windshield

Details: a small branch fell from a tree and cracked the windshield of waste collection truck No. 284673NYC.

-----

7. Which of the following four versions is most clear, accurate and complete?

A. On September 11, 2019, in front of 1726 West 8ᵗʰ Street, Brooklyn, a small branch fell from a tree and cracked the windshield of waste collection truck No. 284678NYC, driven by Sanitation Worker Charles Broom.

B. On September 11, 2019, in front of 1726 West 8ᵗʰ Street, Brooklyn, a small branch fell from a tree and cracked the windshield of waste collection truck No. 284673NYC, driven by Sanitation Worker Charles Broom.

C. On September 11, 2019, at 12:25 p.m., in front of 1726 West 8ᵗʰ Street, Brooklyn, a small branch fell from a tree and cracked the windshield of waste collection truck No. 284673NYC, driven by Sanitation Worker Charles Droom.

D. On September 11, 2019, at 12:25 P.M., in front of 1726 West 8ᵗʰ Street, Brooklyn, a small branch fell from a tree and cracked the windshield of waste collection truck No. 284673NYC, driven by Sanitation Worker Charles Broom.

<u>**Written Expression Answer 7**</u>

Sanitation Worker Able is asked to select the best summary (A, B, C or D) of the following information: (The best summary is the one that expresses the information in the **most clear, accurate and complete manner**).

Place of accident: in front of 1726 West 8th Street., Brooklyn

Time of accident: 12:25 P.M.

Date of accident: September 11, 2019

Vehicle involved: waste collection truck No. 284673NYC

Sanitation Worker Driver: Charles Broom

Damage: cracked windshield

Details: a small branch fell from a tree and cracked the windshield of waste collection truck No. 284673NYC.

-----

7. Which of the following four versions is most clear, accurate and complete?

A. On September 11, 2019, in front of 1726 West 8th Street, Brooklyn, a small branch fell from a tree and cracked the windshield of waste collection truck No. 28467**8**NYC, driven by Sanitation Worker: Charles Broom.
   (**WRONG** because the time of the accident is not stated and the waste collection truck number 28467**8**NYC is not correct.)

B. On September 11, 2019, in front of 1726 West 8th Street, Brooklyn, a small branch fell from a tree and cracked the windshield of waste collection truck No. 284673NYC, driven by Sanitation Worker: Charles Broom.
   (**WRONG** because the time of the accident is not stated.)

C. On September 11, 2019, at 12:25 p.m., in front of 1726 West 8th Street, Brooklyn, a small branch fell from a tree and cracked the windshield of waste collection truck No. 284673NYC, driven by Sanitation Worker: Charles **Droom**.
   (**WRONG** because the last name of the driver is misspelled "**Dr**oom.")

D. <u>**On September 11, 2019, at 12:25 P.M., in front of 1726 West 8th Street, Brooklyn, a small branch fell from a tree and cracked the windshield of waste collection truck No. 284673NYC, driven by Sanitation Worker Charles Broom.**</u>
   (**THIS IS THE CORRECT ANSWER.** It contains all the information and does not have any factual errors.)

Written Expression Question 8

Sanitation Worker Harry Garlin has collected the following information regarding a traffic accident in which he was involved while on duty. Which is the best summary?

Date of accident: July 4, 2019
Time of accident: 2:25 P.M.
Place of accident: intersection of 5th Avenue and 48th Street, Staten Island
Vehicles involved: NYC Sanitation Dept. truck , plate # A78275T and a 2007 Nissan,
               plate # TH748GVK
Drivers: Harry Garlin (NYC Sanitation Dept. truck) and Jeff Norquist (2007 Nissan)
Damage: dent on driver's door of 2007 Nissan

-----

8. Sanitation Worker Harry Garlin needs to quickly report the above information to his supervisor. He drafts four versions to express the above information. Which of the following four versions is most clear, accurate and complete?

A. On July 4, 2019, at 2:52 P.M., at the intersection of 5th Avenue and 48th Street, Staten Island, a NYC Sanitation Dept. truck , plate # A78275T, driven by me, and a 2007 Nissan, plate # TH748GVK, were involved in a traffic accident. The 2007 Nissan, driven by Jeff Norquist, sustained a dent on the driver's door. The Sanitation Dept. vehicle did not sustain any damage.

B. On July 4, 2019, at 2:25 P.M., at the intersection of 5th Avenue and 48th Street, Staten Island, a NYC Sanitation Dept. truck , plate # A78275T, driven by me, and a 2007 Nissan, plate # TH748GVR, were involved in a traffic accident. The 2007 Nissan, driven by Jeff Norquist, sustained a dent on the driver's door. The Sanitation Dept. vehicle did not sustain any damage.

C. On July 4, 2019, at 2:25 P.M., at the intersection of 5th Avenue and 48th Street, Staten Island, a NYC Sanitation Dept. truck, driven by me, and a 2007 Nissan, plate # TH748GVK, were involved in a traffic accident. The 2007 Nissan, driven by Jeff Norquist, sustained a dent on the driver's door. The Sanitation Dept. vehicle did not sustain any damage.

D. On July 4, 2019, at 2:25 P.M., at the intersection of 5th Avenue and 48th Street, Staten Island, a NYC Sanitation Dept. truck , plate # A78275T, driven by Harry Garlin, and a 2007 Nissan, plate # TH748GVK, were involved in a traffic accident. The 2007 Nissan, driven by Jeff Norquist, sustained a dent on the driver's door. The Sanitation Dept. vehicle did not sustain any damage.

Written Expression Answer 8

Sanitation Worker Harry Garlin has collected the following information regarding a traffic accident at which he was involved while on duty. Which is the best summary?

Date of accident: July 4, 2019
Time of accident: 2:25 P.M.
Place of accident: intersection of 5th Avenue and 48th Street, Staten Island
Vehicles involved: NYC Sanitation Dept. truck , plate # A78275T and a 2007 Nissan,
            plate # TH748GVK
Drivers: Harry Garlin (NYC Sanitation Dept. truck) and Jeff Norquist (2007 Nissan)
Damage: dent on driver's door of 2007 Nissan

-----

8. Sanitation Worker Harry Garlin needs to quickly report the above information to his supervisor. He drafts four versions to express the above information. Which of the following four versions is most clear, accurate and complete?

A. On July 4, 2019, at **2:52 P.M.**, at the intersection of 5th Avenue and 48th Street, Staten Island, a NYC Sanitation Dept. truck, plate # A78275T, driven by me, and a 2007 Nissan, plate # TH748GVK, were involved in a traffic accident. The 2007 Nissan, driven by Jeff Norquist, sustained a dent on the driver's door. The Sanitation Dept. vehicle did not sustain any damage. (**NOT CORRECT**. Time is wrong. It is stated as 2:**52** P.M. instead of 2:**25** P.M.)

B. On July 4, 2019, at 2:25 P.M., at the intersection of 5th Avenue and 48th Street, Staten Island, a NYC Sanitation Dept. truck, plate # A78275T, driven by me, and a 2007 Nissan, plate # TH748GV**R**, were involved in a traffic accident. The 2007 Nissan, driven by Jeff Norquist, sustained a dent on the driver's door. The Sanitation Dept. vehicle did not sustain any damage. (**WRONG**: Plate number is wrong. Last letter is "K", not "R.")

C. On July 4, 2019, at 2:25 P.M., at the intersection of 5th Avenue and 48th Street, Staten Island, a NYC Sanitation Dept. truck, driven by me, and a 2007 Nissan, plate # TH748GVK, were involved in a traffic accident. The 2007 Nissan, driven by Jeff Norquist, sustained a dent on the driver's door. The Sanitation Dept. vehicle did not sustain any damage. (**WRONG**. Plate number of NYC Sanitation Dept. truck (**plate # A78275T**) has been left out.)

D. **On July 4, 2019, at 2:25 P.M., at the intersection of 5th Avenue and 48th Street, Staten Island, a NYC Sanitation Dept. truck , plate # A78275T, driven by Harry Garlin, and a 2007 Nissan, plate # TH748GVK, were involved in a traffic accident. The 2007 Nissan, driven by Jeff Norquist, sustained a dent on the driver's door. The Sanitation Dept. vehicle did not sustain any damage**.
(**This is the CORRECT answer.** It contains all the information and does not have any factual errors.)

PROBLEM SENSITIVITY

4

These questions evaluate your ability to see the elements of a problem and also the problem in its entirety.

Problem sensitivity is important in a Sanitation Worker's daily work. Spotting a possible problem developing during a shift may aid the Sanitation Worker in preventing an incident or being ready if it does occur.

This type of question evaluates your ability to analyze different situations using applicable personal experience, problem sensitivity and maturity of thought.

In one version of this type of question, rules or procedures may be presented along with a situation or incident where the stated rules or procedures should be applied.

Another version of this type of question may present a number of "facts" (some conflicting), as stated by different persons. The candidate may be asked which description or account has a problem, or which description or account is the most correct.

Problem Sensitivity Questions 1 - 6

1. During the last few minutes of her daily tour, Sanitation Worker Kimberly Foster is informed by a person that a red liquid which seems like blood is seeping out of a large private company garbage container located next to the side of a building where a shoe store is located. A foul smell is also coming out and has been increasing during the past two days.

Based on the above, Sanitation Worker Kimberly Foster should:

A. not do anything since there are only a few minutes remaining in her daily shift.

B. go to the container, take samples of the liquid and have it analyzed by an independent lab.

C. immediately question all persons on the street.

D. take a look at the container and if the facts are as reported, inform her supervisor.

----

2. Sanitation Worker Elton Turner notices that a huge tree branch has fallen on the sidewalk, next to the front entrance of a city park. He has several traffic cones with him.

Sanitation Worker Turner should:

A. immediately barricade the entrance to the park and thereby decrease the possibility of an accident.

B. immediately barricade both entrances to the street where the tree branch has fallen.

C. call the office of the head of the NYC Parks Department and ask to speak with him directly.

D. report the fallen tree limb to the proper authority.

----

3. During his shift, Sanitation Worker Charles Williams notices that a metal store sign approximately three feet wide and ten feet long has partially detached from a building and is dangerously close to crashing down to the crowded sidewalk, about twenty feet below.

Based on the preceding information, what is the first step that Sanitation Worker Williams should take?

A. Call for another waste collection crew as he is alone.

B. Quickly alert all persons in the vicinity to the danger and notify his supervisor.

C. Look at the sign for at least five minutes to determine when it will fall.

D. Go inside the store and notify the store owner.

4. Before you leave for your waste pick-up route, your supervisor asks that you speak with the owner of a house on your route, a Mr. Mary Franklin, regarding a complaint by the person that two pieces of broken furniture have not been picked up by sanitation during the last two bulk pick-up days. You are confused about the identity (name and gender) of Mr. Mary Franklin.

What is the first step you should take in this situation?

A. At the home of Mr. Mary Franklin speak with anyone named Franklin (male or female).

B. Disregard the supervisor's instructions as they are clearly confused.

C. Do not ask questions of the supervisor, as he might get upset.

D. For ID purposes, ask the supervisor for clarification of the name and gender of the person.

----

5. Sanitation Worker Elaine Marton is working on her sanitation route when she notices a man walking in an apparent daze in front of a private garbage dumpster. Because the man seems like he might collapse, Sanitation Worker Elaine Marton asks him if there is any problem. The man is clearly startled at being asked a question and hurriedly says "I didn't throw the dead cat in the dumpster!" and quickly empties his pants pockets, which contained only a bottle of prescription pills which Sanitation Worker Elaine Marton knows are for anxiety. At that point the man loses consciousness and collapses, but Sanitation Worker Elaine Marton is able to catch him before he falls on the sidewalk.

Based on the preceding information, what should Sanitation Worker Elaine Marton do first?

A. Take the man to the dumpster and ask him where exactly he threw the dead cat.

B. Interview all nearby persons to determine if any are aware of this man throwing a dead cat into the dumpster.

C. Call her supervisor and inform her of the situation and need for medical assistance.

D. Call the local precinct to determine if the man has an arrest record, including cruelty to animals.

----

6. Prior to leaving for your route, your supervisor gives you instructions which due to your distance from him, you do not hear part of the instructions.

What should you do first?

A. Quickly carry-out as many instructions as you can remember.

B. Ask your supervisor to repeat the instructions.

C. After you leave for your route, ask another Sanitation Worker if he heard the instructions.

D. Carry out all instructions that you heard and then call the supervisor to ask him if you have completed all of his instructions.

Problem Sensitivity Answers 1 - 6

1. During the last few minutes of her daily tour, Sanitation Worker Kimberly Foster is informed by a person that a red liquid which seems like blood is seeping out of a large private company garbage container located next to the side of a building where a shoe store is located. A foul smell is also coming out and has been increasing during the past two days.

Based on the above, Sanitation Worker Kimberly Foster should:

A. not do anything since there are only a few minutes remaining in her daily shift.

B. go to the container, take samples of the liquid and have it analyzed by an independent lab.

C. immediately question all persons on the street.

D. **take a look at the container and if the facts are as reported, inform her supervisor**. **(Choice "D" is the correct answer.** Although the garbage container is a private container (and not one that is collected by the NYC Sanitation Department), the possibility exists that the liquid might be real blood (unusual for a container used by a shoe store). As a Sanitation Worker, Ms. Foster should not take it upon herself to conduct an investigation. Although there are only a few minutes left in her shift, she should take a brief look to confirm the allegations of the person and if the facts are as reported, she should promptly notify her supervisor who will take appropriate action.)

----

2. Sanitation Worker Elton Turner notices that a huge tree branch has fallen on the sidewalk, next to the front entrance of a city park. He has several traffic cones with him.

Sanitation Worker Turner should:

A. immediately barricade the entrance to the park and thereby decrease the possibility of an accident.

B. immediately barricade both entrances to the street where the tree branch has fallen.

C. call the office of the head of the NYC Parks Department and ask to speak with him directly.

D. **report the fallen tree limb to the proper authority**

(Choice "D" is the correct answer. Although a tree limb has fallen, there is no indication that there is any emergency. Calling the office of the head of the NYC Parks Department and asking to speak with him directly is completely uncalled for. Mr. Turner should report the fallen tree limb to the proper authority, which may be his supervisor or agency, depending on procedure.)

----

3. During his shift, Sanitation Worker Charles Williams notices that a metal store sign approximately three feet wide and ten feet long has partially detached from a building and is dangerously close to crashing down to the crowded sidewalk, about twenty feet below.

Based on the preceding information, what is the first step that Sanitation Worker Williams should take?

A. Call for another waste collection crew as he is alone.

B. **Quickly alert all persons in the vicinity to the danger and notify his supervisor.**

C. Look at the sign for at least five minutes to determine when it will fall.

D. Go inside the store and notify the store owner.

(Choice "B" is the correct answer. Because the sign is in danger of falling, he should quickly alert all persons in the vicinity to the danger and notify his supervisor. Barricading streets or doing an investigation should be left to the proper authorities. Calling for another crew would not help because the other crew would not have any greater authority than him.)

----

4. Before you leave for your waste pick-up route, your supervisor asks that you speak with the owner of a house on your route, a Mr. Mary Franklin, regarding a complaint by the person that two pieces of broken furniture have not been picked up by sanitation during the last two bulk pick-up days. You are confused about the identity (name and gender) of Mr. Mary Franklin.

What is the first step you should take in this situation?

A. At the home of Mr. Mary Franklin speak with anyone named Franklin (male or female).

  (WRONG) The sanitation worker should get clarification from the supervisor of the correct name before leaving for the route.

B. Disregard the supervisor's instructions as they are clearly confused.

  (WRONG) Orders from a supervisor should not be disregarded.

C. Do not ask questions of the supervisor, as he might get upset.

  (WRONG) Questions should be asked whenever clarification is needed.

D. For ID purposes, <u>**ask the supervisor for clarification of the name and gender of the person**</u>.

  (CORRECT ANSWER) A sanitation worker should ask questions of a superior whenever clarification or additional relevant information is needed.

----

5. Sanitation Worker Elaine Marton is working on her sanitation route when she notices a man walking in an apparent daze in front of a private garbage dumpster. Because the man seems like he might collapse, Sanitation Worker Elaine Marton asks him if there is any problem. The man is clearly startled at being asked a question and hurriedly says "I didn't throw the dead cat in the dumpster!" and quickly empties his pants pockets, which contained only a bottle of prescription pills which Sanitation Worker Elaine Marton knows are for anxiety. At that point the man loses consciousness and collapses, but Sanitation Worker Elaine Marton is able to catch him before he falls on the sidewalk.

Based on the preceding information, what should Sanitation Worker Elaine Marton do first?

A. Take the man to the dumpster and ask him where exactly he threw the dead cat.

  (WRONG) Medical assistance is first required because the man lost consciousness.

B. Interview all nearby persons to determine if any are aware of this man throwing a dead cat into the dumpster.

  (WRONG) Medical assistance is first required.

C. **Call her supervisor and inform her of the situation and need for medical assistance.**

(CORRECT) The man lost consciousness. This is a medical emergency. The correct action to take is to call for medical assistance.

D. Call the local precinct to determine if the man has an arrest record, including cruelty to animals.

(WRONG) Medical assistance is first required. An investigation should be left to the police.

----

6. Prior to leaving for your route, your supervisor gives you instructions which due to your distance from him, you do not hear part of the instructions.

What should you do first?

A. Quickly carry-out as many instructions as you can remember.

(WRONG) You should carry out all instructions from the supervisor, and not just those that you remember.

B. **Ask your supervisor to repeat the instructions.**

(CORRECT) Asking for clarification is correct because this will help you understand all the instructions which you must follow.

C. After you leave for your route, ask another Sanitation Worker if he heard the instructions.

(WRONG) Any clarification should first come from the supervisor.

D. Carry out all instructions that you heard and then call the supervisor to ask him if you have completed all of his instructions.

(WRONG) You should get clarification as soon as possible, in this instance at the time that the supervisor gave the instructions.

_____

"The will to win, the desire to succeed, the urge to reach your full potential... these are the keys that will unlock the door to personal excellence."

-Confucius

INFORMATION ORDERING | 5

"The questions may involve "following correctly a rule or set of rules or actions in a certain order. The rule or set of rules must be given. The things or actions to be put in order can include numbers, letters, words, pictures, procedures, sentences, and mathematical or logical operations. This ability may be used to understand the correct order in which a plow must be assembled."[1]

The key to answering this type of question correctly is to make sure that the directions are clear to you.

To obtain maximum clarity, take the time to understand the logical order of the directions. Steps that must be done "before" or "after" or "at the same time" should be noted.

Also, at the time of selecting your answer, refer back to the directions to make sure that you have not mentally mixed up the order or the details of the directions.

The following "Information Ordering" examples are variations of possible types of questions that may be asked.

Information Ordering Question 1

Answer question 1 based on the following bomb threat procedure.

Bomb Threat Procedure

Some bomb threats are received by phone. A Sanitation Worker who receives a bomb threat by phone should do the following in the order given:

1. Stay calm. Do not hang up, even if the caller hangs up. Be polite and show interest in what the caller is saying.

2. If possible, write a message to a fellow Sanitation Worker or other NYC employee.

3. If your phone displays the caller number, write down the number.

4. Even if the caller hangs up, do not hang up your phone. Use a different phone that is not a cell phone to contact the "Bomb Threat Notification Unit."

5. As soon as possible, complete the "Bomb Threat Checklist."

----

1. At a "Bomb Threat Exercise" conducted at the local Sanitation Office, you are given the following scenario: You are told that you have answered a phone call during which a bomb threat is made. You have written a note and notified a Sanitation Worker who is at the desk next to yours. You have also written down the caller's number which displayed on your phone unit. The caller hangs up.

The next step you should take is to:

A. Hang up the phone and immediately call the "Bomb Threat Notification Unit."

B. Do not hang up the phone. Use a cell phone to contact the "Bomb Threat Notification Unit."

C. Complete the form "Bomb Threat Checklist."

D. Do not hang up and use a different phone (not a cell phone) to contact the "Bomb Threat Notification Unit."

Information Ordering Answer 1

Bomb Threat Procedure

Some bomb threats are received by phone. A Sanitation Worker who receives a bomb threat by phone should do the following in the order given:

1. Stay calm. Do not hang up, even if the caller hangs up. Be polite and show interest in what the caller is saying.

2. If possible, write a message to a fellow Sanitation Worker or other NYC employee.

3. If your phone displays the caller number, write down the number.

4. Even if the caller hangs up, do **not hang up your phone. Use a different phone that is not a cell phone to contact the "Bomb Threat Notification Unit."**

5. As soon as possible, complete the "Bomb Threat Checklist."

----

1. At a "Bomb Threat Exercise" conducted at the local Sanitation Office, you are given the following scenario: You are told that you have answered a phone call during which a bomb threat is made. You have written a note and notified a Sanitation Worker who is at the desk next to yours. You have also written down the caller's number which displayed on your phone unit. The caller hangs up.

The next step you should take is to:

A. Hang up the phone and immediately call the "Bomb Threat Notification Unit."

   WRONG: Number 1 states, "Do **not** hang up..."

B. Do not hang up the phone, but use a cell phone to contact "Bomb Threat Notification Unit."

   WRONG: Number 3 states, "Use a different phone that is **not** a cell phone..."

C. Complete the form "Bomb Threat Checklist."

   WRONG: Number 5 states, "complete the form "Bomb Threat Checklist." This is the **last** step and is done **after** contacting the "Bomb Threat Notification Unit."

D. **Do not hang up and use a different phone (not a cell phone) to contact the "Bomb Threat Notification Unit." CORRECT:** This is step number four and comes directly after ep number three, "...write down the number."

Information Ordering Question 2

Your supervisor gives you five "Request for Special Pick-Up" forms submitted by residents on your pick-up route. The forms were submitted by the following five persons:

George Felder, Harriet Volker, Ben Halston, Abe Johnson, Diane Molton

He asks you to organize the forms in last name alphabetical order and that you pick up the recycle in that order.

According to the above, the fourth pick-up would be "Request for Special Pick-Up" submitted by:

A. Halston, Ben

B. Volker, Harriet

C. Molton, Diane

D. Felder, George

Information Ordering Answer 2

The correct listing in last name alphabetical order is:

1) Felder, George

2) Halston, Ben

3) Johnson, Abe

4) Molton, Diane

5) Volker, Harriet

The fourth name on the list is Molton, Diane, therefore the correct answer is **C) Molton, Diane**.

Information Ordering Questions 3 and 4

A Sanitation Worker who is assigned to drive a department vehicle may be involved in a motor vehicle accident with another vehicle. When such an accident occurs, the Sanitation Worker must use good judgment and follow established department procedural guidelines. These guidelines include the following five guidelines which are listed in random order and not in priority order.

1. Record names of parties and witnesses to the accident.

2. Fill out all required Sanitation Department forms to record the case information.

3. Report incident to Sanitation Department Headquarters and call 911 if necessary.

4. Record any assistance from police or other agencies, including ambulance information.

5. Determine if any life-saving assistance is needed, and if possible render assistance.

3. What is the logical order for the above motor vehicle accident procedures?

A. 2, 3, 1, 4, 5

B. 1, 5, 3, 4, 2

C. 3, 1, 4, 2, 5

D. 5, 3, 1, 4, 2

Information Ordering Answer 3

3. Answer: D. 5, 3, 1, 4, 2

5. Determine if any life-saving assistance is needed, and if possible render assistance.

3. Report incident to Sanitation Department Headquarters and call 911 if necessary.

1. Record names of parties and witnesses to the accident.

4. Record any assistance from police or other agencies, including ambulance information.

2. Fill out all required Sanitation Department forms to record the case information.

Information Ordering Question 4

4. Which of the above five steps is logically the last step that should be done by the Sanitation Worker driver that is involved in a motor vehicle accident?

A. Step one

B. Step five

C. Step three

D. none of the above

Information Ordering Answer 4

4. Answer: B. Step five

Information Ordering Question 5

Procedure for waste bags pickup at one and two family unit buildings

A Sanitation Worker who is assigned to a garbage collection vehicle must follow department guidelines for garbage pickup at one and two family unit buildings. These guidelines include the following five guidelines which are listed in random order and not in priority order.

1. Determine whether the number of waste bags is within the maximum six bag limit per family.

2. If any waste appears to be biohazard waste, immediately report that fact by radio to the local area supervisor.

3. If the number of waste bags exceeds the maximum limit per family, only pick up six bags per family and leave a notice on the household door informing them of the six bag limit.

4. Upon arrival at the building, visually inspect the refuse to determine if it meets proper refuse public safety guidelines.

5. After determining that no waste is hazardous, refer to the department address listing to determine whether the address is a one or two family address.

Question 5

5. What is the logical order for the above Procedure for waste bags pickup at one and two family unit buildings?

A. 1, 2, 5, 3, 4

B. 2, 4, 5, 1 ,3

C. 4, 2, 5, 1, 3

D. 4, 2, 5, 3, 1

5. Answer: C. 4, 2, 5, 1, 3

4. Upon arrival at the building, visually inspect the refuse to determine if it meets proper refuse public safety guidelines.

2. If any waste appears to be biohazard waste, immediately report that fact by radio to the local area supervisor.

5. After determining that no waste is hazardous, refer to the department address listing to determine whether the address is a one or two family address.

1. Determine whether the number of waste bags is within the maximum six bag limit per family.

3. If the number of waste bags exceeds the maximum limit per family, only pick up six bags per family and leave a notice on the household door informing them of the six bag limit.

Information Ordering Question 6

Organize the following four sentences in the best logical order:

1. This training includes classroom and "on the street" practice driving.

2. Because of this, they receive proper driving and safety instruction.

3. "On the street" driving is stressed and comprises eighty percent of the training time.

4. Sanitation Workers may be assigned to drive a waste collection vehicle.

(A) 1, 3, 4, 2

(B) 2, 3, 4, 1

(C) 3, 2, 1, 4

(D) 4, 2, 1, 3

Information Ordering Answer 6

The correct answer is **(D) 4, 2, 1, 3**.

4. Sanitation Workers may be assigned to drive a waste collection vehicle.

   (This sentence introduces the topic of driving waste collection vehicles.)

2. Because of this, they receive proper driving and safety instruction.

1. This training includes classroom and "on the street" practice driving.

3. "On the street" driving is stressed and comprises eighty percent of the training time.

Information Ordering Question 7

Your supervisor hands you five "Overtime Request Forms" which you submitted for payment. He reminds you that all overtime requests must be submitted in date order and numbered sequentially. The dates on the overtime forms are as follows:

10-4-2019   9/24/2019   October 1, 2019   September 28, 2019   Sept. 12, 2019

He asks you to number the forms in ascending date order and that you resubmit them again. Assuming that you organize the forms as your supervisor asks and number the first request "Request 1," which of the above dated requests would be numbered "Request 3"?

A. 10-4-2019

B. 9/24/2019

C. October 1, 2019

D. September 28, 2019

Information Ordering Answer 7

The correct ascending date order is:

      1) Sept. 12, 2019

      2) 9/24/2019

      3) September 28, 2019

      4) October 1, 2019

      5) 10-4-2019

The third date on the list is September 28, 2019. Therefore, the correct answer is **D**.

Information Ordering Question 8

The following are four sentences. Each sentence (listed in random order) is one of the four steps necessary to attach a snow plow to the front of a truck. Which one of the following choices (A, B, C, D) lists the order of sentences which best expresses the logical sequence of snow plow installation?

    1. Drive truck slowly forward to test whether the plow is securely bolted to the truck.

    2. Tighten the bolts with heavy duty nuts.

    3. Align the front of the truck with the snow plow connectors.

    4. Insert connecting bolts in aligned holes of snow plow and the truck's snow plow connector.

A. 1, 4, 2, 3

B. 2, 3, 4, 1

C. 4, 1, 3, 2

D. 3, 4, 2, 1

Information Ordering Answer 8

The correct answer is **D. 3, 4, 2, 1**

3. Align the front of the truck with the snow plow connectors.

4. Insert connecting bolts in aligned holes of snow plow and the truck's snow plow connector.

2. Tighten the bolts with heavy duty nuts.

1. Drive truck slowly forward to test whether the plow is securely bolted to the truck.

DEDUCTIVE REASONING

6

These questions evaluate your ability to understand general rules and apply them to specific situations.

Sometimes a question of this type may be difficult to answer, especially when the question involves a detailed procedure or set of instructions.

When answering a question of this type, try to understand fully the procedure or set of instructions. More than one reading may be necessary. As you read, try to see the relationships among the details provided.

Keep in mind that although it may be possible to answer very quickly some questions in other sections of the exam, the questions in this section may require more concentration and time.

Deductive Reasoning Questions 1 - 3

Answer question 1 - 3 based on the information provided in the following "Non-Commercial Waste Collection Procedure."

General Non-Commercial Waste Collection Procedure

1. Garbage containers, recycle containers and bulk items must be at curbside before 7:00 A.M. on the scheduled collection day.
2. Only garbage containers meeting HMA Standards are acceptable. Contents of garbage containers that do not meet HMA Standards will not be picked up.
3. Garbage must be household waste only.
4. The following will need a special commercial pick-up appointment and will not be picked up on regular pick-up days: building/demolition materials of any type, including garage doors, shingles, construction lumber, textiles and fixtures.
5. The following items must be separated and placed in appropriate recycle containers: newspapers, cardboard, junk mail, aluminum beverage cans, metal and tin cans, plastic bottles and jars and leaves.
6. Cans that are obstructed will not be collected.
7. Bulk items will not be picked up on regular collection days.*

-----

1. Based on the above "Non-Commercial Waste Collection Procedure," which of the following statements is correct?
A. Garbage containers may contain non household waste.
B. Garbage containers that are used solely for household waste may be non HMA compliant.
C. Plastic bottles do not have to be separated for collection.
D. On regular collection days bulk items will not be picked up.

----

2. According to the "Non-Commercial Waste Collection Procedure":
A. Cans that are obstructed will be collected.
B. Garbage must be commercial waste only.
C. Bulk items will be picked up on regular collection days.
D. Garage doors need a special commercial pick-up appointment.

3. Based on the above "Non-Commercial Waste Collection Procedure," which of the following statements is not correct?

A. The following items must be separated and placed in appropriate recycle containers: newspapers, cardboard, junk mail, aluminum beverage cans, metal and tin cans, plastic bottles and jars and leaves.

B. Garbage containers, recycle containers and bulk items must be at curbside before 7:00 P.M. on the scheduled collection day.

C. Garbage must be household waste only.

D. Only garbage containers meeting HMA Standards are acceptable. Contents of garbage containers that do not meet HMA Standards will not be picked up.

Deductive Reasoning Answers 1 - 3

Answer question 1 - 3 based on the information provided in the following "Non-Commercial Waste Collection Procedure."

Non-Commercial Waste Collection Procedure

1. Garbage containers, recycle containers and bulk items must be at curbside before <u>7:00 A.M.</u> on the scheduled collection day.

2. Only garbage containers meeting HMA Standards are acceptable. Contents of garbage containers that do not meet <u>HMA Standards</u> will not be picked up.

3. Garbage must be <u>household</u> waste only.

4. The following will need a special commercial pick-up appointment and will not be picked up on regular pick-up days: building/demolition materials of any type, including <u>garage doors</u>, shingles, construction lumber, textiles and fixtures.

5. The following items <u>must be separated</u> and placed in appropriate recycle containers: newspapers, cardboard, junk mail, aluminum beverage cans, metal and tin cans, plastic bottles and jars and leaves.

6. Cans that are obstructed will <u>not</u> be collected.

7. <u>Bulk items will not be picked up on regular collection days</u>.*

-----

1. Based on the above "Non-Commercial Waste Collection Procedure," which of the following statements is <u>correct</u>?

A. Garbage containers may contain non household waste.

   (**WRONG**. "3. Garbage must be **household** waste only.")

B. Garbage containers that are used solely for household waste may be non HMA compliant.

   (**WRONG**. "Only garbage containers meeting HMA Standards are acceptable. Contents of garbage containers that do not meet HMA Standards will not be picked up.")

C. Plastic bottles do not have to be separated for collection.

   (**WRONG**. "5. The following items must be separated and placed in appropriate recycle containers: newspapers, cardboard, junk mail, aluminum beverage cans, metal and tin cans, **plastic bottles** and jars and leaves.")

D. <u>On regular collection days bulk items will not be picked up</u>.

   (**CORRECT. THIS IS THE ANSWER.** "7. Bulk items will not be picked up on regular collection days.")

----

2. According to the "Non-Commercial Waste Collection Procedure:"

A. Cans that are obstructed will be collected.

   (**WRONG**. "6. Cans that are obstructed will **not** be collected.")

B. Garbage must be commercial waste only.

   (**WRONG**. "3. Garbage must be **household** waste only.")

C. Bulk items will be picked up on regular collection days.

   (**WRONG**. "7. Bulk items will **not** be picked up on regular collection days.")

D. <u>Garage doors need a special commercial pick-up appointment</u>.

   (**CORRECT. THIS IS THE ANSWER.** "4. The following will need a special commercial pick-up appointment and will not be picked up on regular pick-up days: building/demolition materials of any type, including <u>garage doors</u>, shingles, construction lumber, textiles and fixtures.")

----

3. Based on the above "Non-Commercial Waste Collection Procedure," which of the following statements is <u>not</u> correct?

A. The following items must be separated and placed in appropriate recycle containers: newspapers, cardboard, junk mail, aluminum beverage cans, metal and tin cans, plastic bottles and jars and leaves. (**CORRECT**)

B. <u>**Garbage containers, recycle containers and bulk items must be at curbside before 7:00 P.M. on the scheduled collection day.**</u>

   (**NOT CORRECT. THIS IS THE ANSWER.** The correct time is 7:00 <u>A.M.</u>, and not 7:00 <u>P.M.</u>)

C. Garbage must be household waste only.

   (**CORRECT**)

D. Only garbage containers meeting HMA Standards are acceptable. Contents of garbage containers that do not meet HMA Standards will not be picked up.

   (**CORRECT**.)

Deductive Reasoning Questions 4 - 6

Answer question 4 - 6 based on the information provided in the following "Recycle Waste Procedures."

Recycle Waste Procedures

The following will only be picked up on special collection days:

Tree Leaves and grass clippings

Organic Garden Refuse (not including stones, bricks and plastic and metal objects)

Brush Or Tree Limbs

The following will be picked up on regular collection days, but must be placed in the following colored containers:

Blue containers:	Red containers:	Green Containers:
Newspapers	Aluminum Beverage Cans	Plastic Bottles
cardboard	Metal and Tin Cans	Glass Bottles
paper		

-----

4. Which of the following statements is correct?

A. Aluminum beverage cans must be placed in blue containers.

B. Grass clippings will be picked up on regular collection days.

C. Tree limbs will be picked up on special collection days.

D. Glass bottles will be picked up on special collection days.

----

5. Which one of the following choices contains one item which should not be placed in the stated container?

A. tin cans, metal, and aluminum beverage cans in red containers

B. in blue containers: paper, cardboard, newspapers, plastic bottles

C. glass bottles in green containers

D. newspapers in blue containers

----

6. Which of the following contains at least one item that is not picked up on regular collection days?

A. newspapers, cardboard, paper, aluminum beverage cans

B. metal and tin cans, plastic bottles, glass bottles, cardboard

C. metal and tin cans, plastic bottles, newspapers, paper

D. cardboard, paper, aluminum beverage cans, grass clippings

_____

Deductive Reasoning Answers 4 - 6

4. Which of the following statements is correct?

A. Aluminum beverage cans must be placed in blue containers.

   (**WRONG**. "**Red** containers: **Aluminum Beverage Cans**, Metal and Tin Cans.")

B. Grass clippings will be picked up on regular collection days.

   (**WRONG**. "The following will only be picked up on **special** collection days: Tree Leaves and **grass clippings**.")

C. **Tree limbs will be picked up on special collection days.**

   (**CORRECT. THIS IS THE ANSWER.** "The following will only be picked up on special collection days: Tree Leaves and grass clippings, Organic Garden Refuse (not including stones, bricks and plastic and metal objects, Brush Or Tree Limbs.")

D. Glass bottles will be picked up on special collection days.

   (**WRONG**. "The following will be picked up on **regular** collection days, but must be placed in the following colored containers... Green Containers: Plastic Bottles, **Glass Bottles**.")

----

5. Which one of the following choices contains one item which should not be placed in the stated container?

A. tin cans, metal, and aluminum beverage cans in red containers

   (**List is correct**.)

B. **in blue containers: paper, card board, newspapers, plastic bottles**

   (**THIS IS THE ANSWER.** It contains one item (plastic bottles) that should NOT be placed in blue containers. They should be placed in green containers.)

C. glass bottles in green containers (**List is correct**.)

D. newspapers in blue containers (**List is correct**.)

----

6. Which of the following contains at least one item that is not picked up on regular collection days?

A. newspapers, cardboard, paper, aluminum beverage cans

B. metal and tin cans, plastic bottles, glass bottles, cardboard

C. metal and tin cans, plastic bottles, newspapers, paper

D. **cardboard, paper, aluminum beverage cans, grass clippings**

   ("The following will only be picked up on special collection days: Tree Leaves and grass clippings.")

Questions 7 and 8 are based on the following map. In answering the questions, follow the flow of traffic, as indicated by the arrows. Names of streets, buildings, public areas, and points 1-9 are indicated on the map.

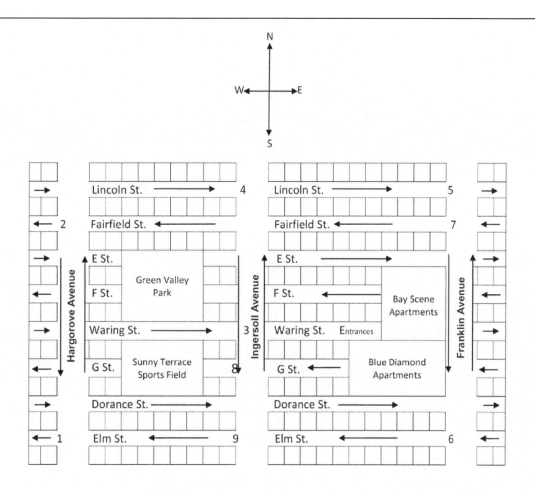

7. Imagine that you are at Elm Street and Ingersoll Avenue and then drive West to Hargrove Avenue, then turn North to Dorance St., then travel East to Ingersoll Avenue, then travel North to Lincoln St. you will be closest to which one of the following points?

A. 2   B. 4   C. 5   D. 7

8. If you start your drive at point number 6, then drive West to Ingersoll Avenue, then drive North to Dorance St., then East to Franklin Avenue, then drive North to Fairfield St., you will be closest to which one of the following points?

A. 4   B. 5   C. 7   D. 2

Answer for Question 7

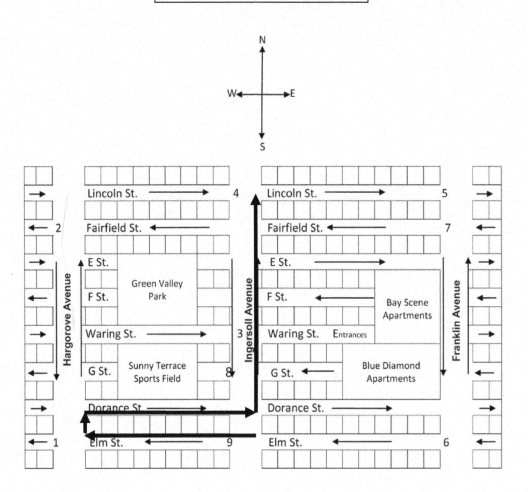

7. Imagine that you are at Elm Street and Ingersoll Avenue and then drive West to Hargrove Avenue, then turn North to Dorance St., then travel East to Ingersoll Avenue, then travel North to Lincoln St. you will be closest to which one of the following points?

A. 2   **B. 4**   C. 5   D. 7

(Route is indicated by dark arrow lines.)

Answer for Question 8

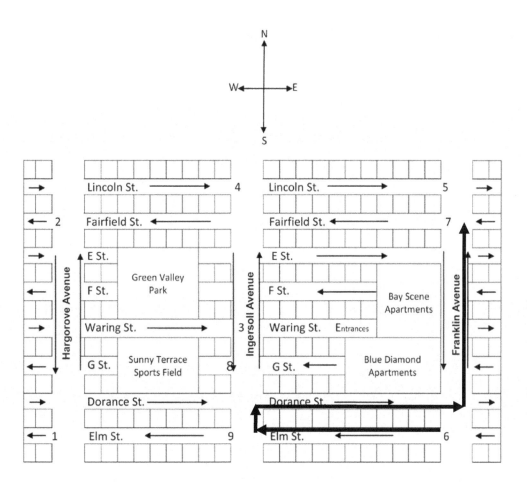

8. If you start your drive at point number 6, then drive West to Ingersoll Avenue, then drive North to Dorance St., then East to Franklin Avenue, then drive North to Fairfield St., you will be closest to which one of the following points?

A. 4   B. 5   **C. 7**   D. 2

(Route is indicated by dark arrow lines.)

Deductive Reasoning Questions 9-11

Answer questions 9 and 10 based on the preceding map.

9. You are in your waste collection truck at the intersection of Lincoln St. and Ingersoll Avenue. You are informed that you are to do a waste collection at the intersection of Lincoln St. and Hargrove Avenue.

Assuming that you must obey all traffic signs, which one of the following four choices describes the most direct route?

A. Drive straight West to the intersection of Lincoln St. and Hargrove Avenue, one block away.

B. Drive East to Franklin Avenue, then South on Franklin Avenue to Fairfield Street, then West on Fairfield St. to Hargrove Avenue, then North on Hargrove Avenue to the intersection of Lincoln St. and Hargrove Avenue.

C. Drive straight East to the intersection of Lincoln St. and Hargrove Avenue, one block away.

D. Drive South on Ingersoll Avenue to Fairfield St, then drive West on Fairfield St. to Hargrove Avenue, then North to the intersection of Lincoln St. and Hargrove Avenue.

----

10. You are in your vehicle at Hargrove Avenue and E St. You are informed that you are to proceed to Lincoln St. and Franklin Avenue where you will pick up two Sanitation Workers.

Which one of the following four choices describes the most direct route?

A. Drive East on Lincoln St. to the corner of Lincoln St. and Franklin Avenue.

B. Drive South to Lincoln St. then right on Lincoln St. to the corner of Lincoln St. and Franklin Avenue.

C. Drive South to Lincoln St. then right on Lincoln St. to the corner of Lincoln St. and Franklin Avenue.

D. Drive North to Lincoln St. then right on Lincoln St. to the corner of Lincoln St. and Franklin Avenue.

Answer question 11 based on the following information:

During the month of July 2019 there were 9 reports by Sanitation Workers that commercial refuse (which is not collected by the NYC Sanitation Department) had been mixed with household refuse. In your collection area there were several reports that a "black van with a severely dented rear bumper" was dumping commercial refuse in front of houses. Some of the witnesses described the van as "dust covered" and probably not washed for weeks. One ss described the driver as a male. One witness described the driver as a female.

11. During the day you notice six different black vans in the area.

Which piece of information should you consider the most important and pay careful attention to in identifying the suspected violator?

A. the black van.

B. male driving a black van.

C. a person driving a black van.

D. a black van with a severe dent in the rear bumper.

"I know the price of success: dedication, hard work and an unremitting devotion to the things you want to see happen."

- Frank Lloyd Wright

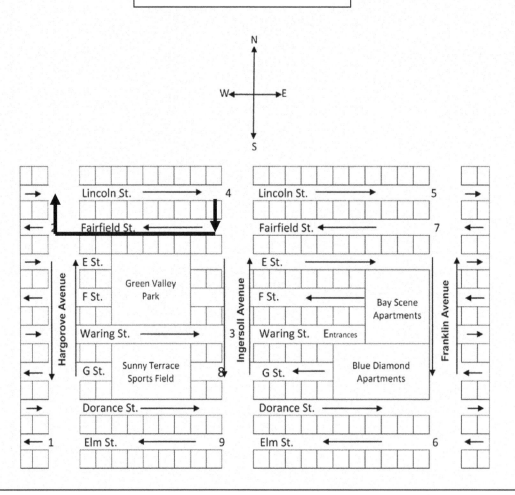

Answer for Question 9

9. You are in your waste collection truck at the intersection of Lincoln St. and Ingersoll Avenue. You are informed that a you are to do a waste collection at the intersection of Lincoln St. and Hargrove Avenue. Assuming that you must obey all traffic signs, which one of the following four choices describes the most direct route?

A. Drive straight West to the intersection of Lincoln St. and Hargrove Avenue, one block away.

B. Drive East to Franklin Avenue, then South on Franklin Avenue to Fairfield Street, then West on Fairfield St. to Hargrove Avenue, then North on Hargrove Avenue to the intersection of Lincoln St. and Hargrove Avenue.

C. Drive straight East to the intersection of Lincoln St. and Hargrove Avenue, one block away.

D. Drive South on Ingersoll Avenue to Fairfield St, then drive West on Fairfield St. to Hargrove Avenue, then North to the intersection of Lincoln St. and Hargrove Avenue.

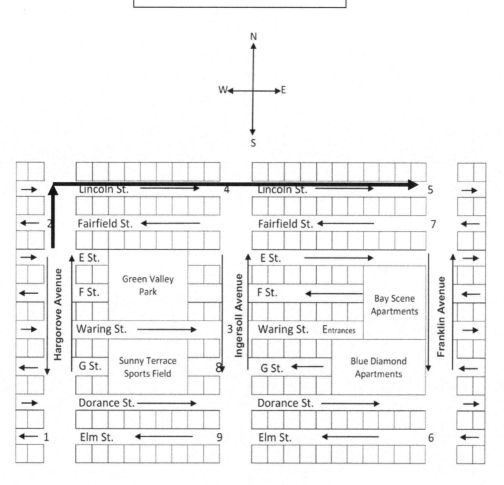

Answer for Question 10

10. You are in your vehicle at Hargrove Avenue and E St. You are informed that you are to proceed to Lincoln St. and Franklin Avenue where you will pick up two Sanitation Workers. Which one of the following four choices describes the most direct route?

A. Drive East on Lincoln St. to the corner of Lincoln St. and Franklin Avenue.

B. Drive South to Lincoln St. then right on Lincoln St. to the corner of Lincoln St. and Franklin Avenue.

C. Drive South to Lincoln St. then right on Lincoln St. to the corner of Lincoln St. and Franklin Avenue.

D. Drive North to Lincoln St. then right on Lincoln St. to the corner of Lincoln St. and Franklin Avenue.

Deductive Reasoning Answer 11

Answer question 11 based on the following information:

During the month of July 2019 there were 9 reports by Sanitation Workers that commercial refuse (which is not collected by the NYC Sanitation Department) had been mixed with household refuse. In your collection area there were several reports that a "black van with a severely dented rear bumper" was dumping commercial refuse in front of houses. Some of the witnesses described the van as "dust covered" and probably not washed for weeks. One witness described the driver as a male. One witness described the driver as a female.

11. During the day you notice six different black vans in the area. Which piece of information should you consider the most important and pay careful attention to in identifying the suspected violator?

A. the black van.

   (**NOT CORRECT**. There are many black vans. More specific description is needed.)

B. male driving a black van.

   (**NOT CORRECT**. The witnesses described a man and a woman. Also, there are many black vans. More specific description is needed.)

C. a person driving a black van.

   (**NOT CORRECT**. This description is not specific enough.)

D. **a black van with a severe dent in the rear bumper.**

   (**THIS IS THE ANSWER.** The severe dent in the bumper, along with the color of the van give enough specific information to eliminate suspecting innocent people while possibly locating the alleged violator.)

"Choose a job that you love and you will never have to work a day in your life."

   - *Confucius*

SPATIAL ORIENTATION

7

These questions evaluate your ability to determine your location and the location of an object with respect to you.

For this type of question, try to keep in mind the following North-East-South-West directional diagram.

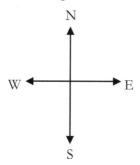

Suggestion: As you read the directional information provided, draw the route as shown in the answers provided for these types of questions.

Spatial Orientation Questions 1 – 3

1. You start your route at East 25 Street and Spencer Avenue. You drive for one block northbound to the end of the block where you make a right turn. You then continue to drive for two blocks before turning right again.

According to the information in the preceding passage, you would be most correct to radio your supervisor that you are heading in which direction?

A) North   B) South   C) East   D) West

----

2. While in your assigned vehicle, you notice a car with what seems to be a teenage driver throwing glass bottle out of the car window. You are behind the car as it drives southbound. After six blocks it makes a right turn and then after two more blocks makes a left turn.

According to the information in the preceding passage, you would be most correct to radio that you last saw the car heading:

A) North   B) South   C) East   D) West

----

3. You drive eastbound for three blocks, then make a right turn and drive for two more blocks before making another right turn.

According to the information in the preceding passage, you would be most correct to radio that you are heading:

A) North   B) South   C) East   D) West

Spatial Orientation Answers 1 – 3

1. You start your route at East 25 Street and Spencer Avenue. You drive for one block northbound to the end of the block where you make a right turn. You then continue to drive for two blocks before turning right again.

According to the information in the preceding passage, you would be most correct to radio your supervisor that you are heading in which direction?

A) North   **B) South**

C) East   D) West

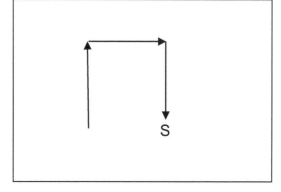

-----

2. While in your assigned vehicle, you notice a car with what seems to be a teenage driver throwing glass bottle out of the car window. You are behind the car as it drives southbound. After six blocks it makes a right turn and then after two more blocks makes a left turn.

According to the information in the preceding passage, you would be most correct to radio that you last saw the car heading:

A) North   **B) South**

C) East   D) West

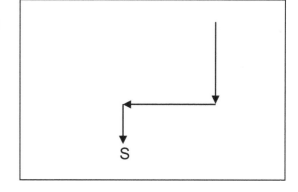

-----

3. You drive eastbound for three blocks, then make a right turn and drive for two more blocks before making another right turn.

According to the information in the preceding passage, you would be most correct to radio that you are heading:

A) North   B) South

C) East   **D) West**

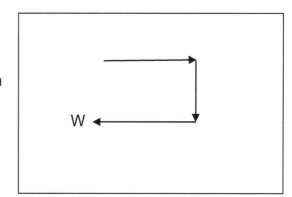

Spatial Orientation Questions 4 – 6

4. Your supervisor asks you to drive your street sweeper in your area and service streets "as needed." From the point where you drive away from your supervisor, you drive in an eastbound direction for two blocks before you turn right and then drive for another block, at which point you turn left.

According to the information in the preceding passage, you would be most correct to radio that you are driving:

A) North   B) South   C) East   D) West

----

5. At the beginning of your daily route, you drive southbound for six blocks, they make a right turn and then after two more blocks you make another right turn.

According to the information in the preceding passage, you would be most correct to radio that you are now heading:

A) North   B) South   C) East   D) West

----

6. You drive in an eastbound direction for three blocks, then make a right turn and drive for two more blocks before making another right turn.

According to the information in the preceding passage, you would be most correct to radio that you are now heading:

A) North   B) South   C) East   D) West

Spatial Orientation Answers 4 - 6

4. Your supervisor asks you to drive your street sweeper in your area and service streets "as needed." From the point where you drive away from your supervisor, you drive in an eastbound direction for two blocks before you turn right and then drive for another block, at which point you turn left.

According to the information in the preceding passage, you would be most correct to radio that you are driving:

A) North   B) South

C) East   D) West

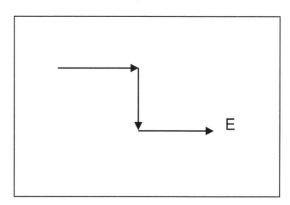

-----

5. At the beginning of your daily route, you drive southbound for six blocks, they make a right turn and then after two more blocks you make another right turn.

According to the information in the preceding passage, you would be most correct to radio that you are now heading:

A) North   B) South

C) East   D) West

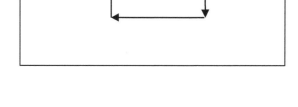

-----

6. You drive in an eastbound direction for three blocks, then make a right turn and drive for two more blocks before making another right turn.

According to the information in the preceding passage, you would be most correct to radio that you are now heading:

A) North   B) South

C) East   **D) West**

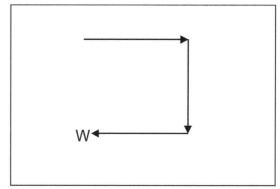

VISUALIZATION

8

These questions evaluate your ability to understand how an object would look when it is rotated or unfolded, or moved in any manner.

When you compare the objects, make point-by-point comparisons. Do not try to compare the object as a whole. If there are differences, they will probably be in the details and not in the main features of the object.

If there are a sequence of objects to be compared (as in the following "Line of crates" example), try to see the pattern and then look at the other examples to see if the pattern is exactly the same or different.

Visualization Question 1

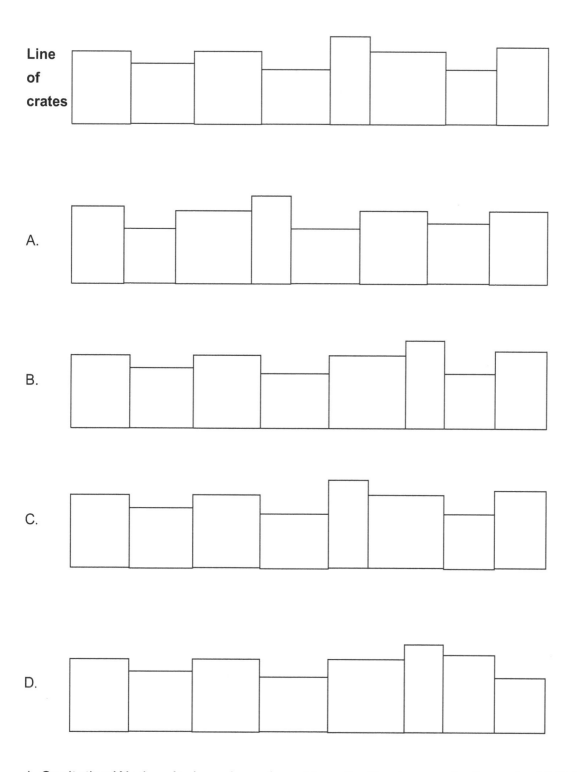

1. Sanitation Worker Jackson is assigned to collecting boxes of refuse at a NYC Facility. He passes a "Line of crates" from the front of the crates. He hears a scratching noise, but keeps on walking. A minute later (when he is several rows behind these crates) he decides to return and investigate. How would the "Line of crates" appear as viewed from the back? (A., B., C. or D?)

Visualization Answer 1

Line
of
crates

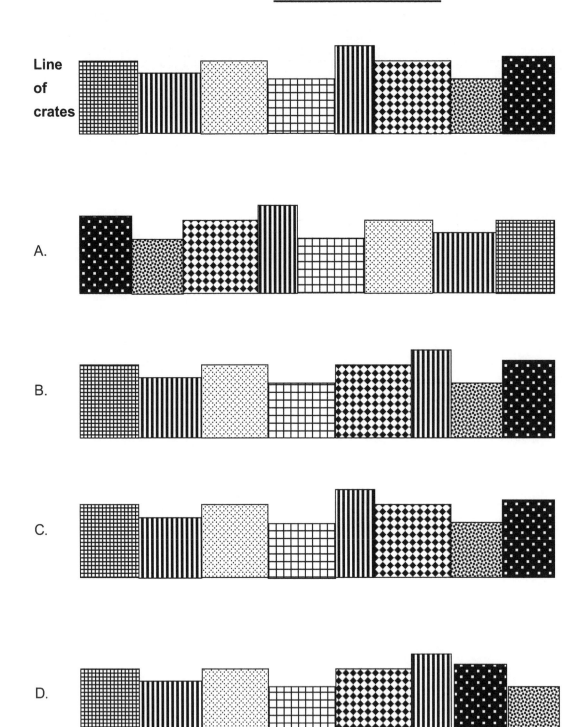

A.

B.

C.

D.

1. The answer is "A."

(To make the answer clear, we have filled in each corresponding box with the same pattern.)

Visualization Question 2

Sanitation Worker Jack Geener is involved in a traffic accident during his daily tour. He is asked by his supervisor to draw a diagram of the accident. (Jack Greener, driver of vehicle #3, stated that he was driving on Hart Avenue when car #1 hit his car from behind, causing him to hit vehicle number 2.) Assume that all 3 vehicles were in their proper lanes of traffic.

Which of the following 4 diagrams below best matches Jack Greener's account?

A   **B**

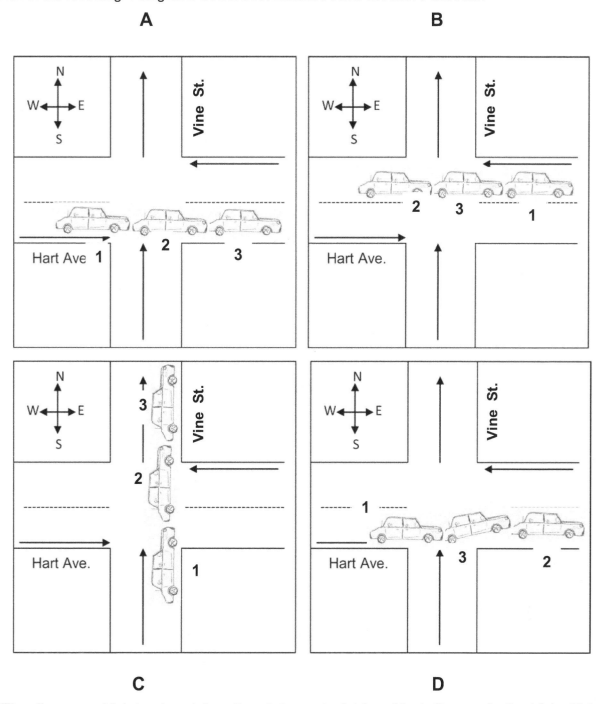

C   **D**

2. The diagram which best matches the statement of driver (Jack Greener) of vehicle #3 is:

A. diagram "A"   C. diagram "

B. diagram "B"   D. diagram "D"

Visualization Answer 2

2. The diagram which best matches the statement of driver (Jack Greener) of vehicle #3 is:

A. diagram "A"
C. diagram "C"

B. diagram "B"
D. diagram "D" (Answer)

Why?

According to the question, "Jack Greener stated that he was driving on Hart Ave. when car #1 hit his car from behind, causing him to hit vehicle number 2."

"Car 1 hits Car 3 which hits Car 2"

1 ⟶ 3 ⟶ 2

The only choice which displays the collision in this sequence and in the proper lane of traffic is choice **"D"**.

Visualization Questions 3 - 5

Answer question 3 based on the following information:

Sanitation Worker John Lagnier collects the following information at the scene of an auto accident involving a NYC Sanitation Department vehicle:

Date of Accident: August 16, 2019

Time of accident: 5:02 p.m.

Place of accident: Intersection of Ferndale Avenue and Willows Avenue, Bronx

Driver: John Lagnier (Sanitation Worker)

Vehicle: 2007 Toyota Sienna (owned by NYC Department of Sanitation)

Damage: Vehicle struck a bicycle partially parked on the sidewalk, but protruding into the street, denting the front bumper of the car.

-----

3. Sanitation Worker John Lagnier is preparing a report of the accident and has four drafts of the report. He wishes to use the draft that expresses the information most clearly, accurately and completely. Which draft should he choose?

A. At 5:20 p.m., on August 16, 2019, at the intersection of Ferndale Avenue and Willows ᵊnue, Bronx, a 2007 Toyota Sienna, owned by the NYC Department of Sanitation and driven by John Lagnier (Sanitation Worker) struck a bicycle partially parked on the sidewalk, but protruding into the street.

B. At 5:02 p.m., on August 6, 2019, at the intersection of Ferndale Avenue and Willows Avenue, Bronx, a 2007 Toyota Sienna, owned by the NYC Department of Sanitation and driven by John Lagnier (Sanitation Worker) struck a bicycle partially parked on the sidewalk, but protruding into the street.

C. At 5:02 p.m., on August 16, 2019, at the intersection of Ferndale Street and Willows Avenue, Bronx, a 2007 Toyota Sienna, owned by the NYC Department of Sanitation and driven by John Lagnier (Sanitation Worker) struck a bicycle partially parked on the sidewalk, but protruding into the street.

D. At 5:02 p.m., on August 16, 2019, at the intersection of Ferndale Avenue and Willows Avenue, Bronx, a 2007 Toyota Sienna, owned by the NYC Department of Sanitation and driven by John Lagnier (Sanitation Worker) struck a bicycle partially parked on the sidewalk, but protruding into the street.

Answer question 4 based on the following information:

Sanitation Worker David Larson needs to report the theft of a NYC Department of Sanitation vehicle. He has the following information:

Suspect: Unidentified

Date of crime: August 15, 2019

Time of crime: between 6:20 p.m. and 11:30 p.m.

Crime: theft of NYC Department of Sanitation auto

Vehicle stolen: 2012 Nissan

Owner of car: NYC Department of Sanitation

Place of crime: driveway in front of 167 28th Street, Staten Island

-----

4. Sanitation Worker David Larson is preparing a report of the theft and has prepared four drafts of the report. He wishes to use the draft that expresses the information most clearly, accurately and completely. Which of the following drafts should he choose?

A. On August 15, 2019, at the driveway in front of 167 28th Street, Staten Island, a 2012 Nissan owned by the NYC Department of Sanitation was stolen by an unidentified suspect.

B. On August 15, 2019, between 6:20 p.m. and 11:30 p.m., at the driveway in front of 176 28th

Street, Staten Island, a 2012 Nissan owned by the NYC Department of Sanitation was stolen by an unidentified suspect.

C. On August 15, 2019, between 6:20 p.m. and 11:30 p.m., at the driveway in front of 167 28th Street, Staten Island, a 2012 Nissan owned by the NYC Department of Sanitation was stolen by an unidentified suspect.

D. On August 15, 2019, between 6:20 p.m. and 11:30 p.m., at the driveway in front of 167 28th Street, Staten Island, a Nissan owned by the NYC Department of Sanitation was stolen by an unidentified suspect.

Answer question 5 based on the following procedure:

Where a Sanitation Worker may be called upon to be a witness in a criminal case, the facts of which arose during the Sanitation Worker's work tour, the Sanitation Worker is prohibited from discussing the case with any newspaper, magazine, TV reporters and all other media. Exceptions to this are where:

1. a New York court of competent jurisdiction formally orders the Sanitation Worker to discuss one or more particulars of the case.

2. a NYC authorized Department orders such discussion.

3. the Sanitation Worker is subpoenaed to testify before an authorized NYC, NYS, or federal board.

-----

5. Sanitation Worker Elaine Homes witnessed the kidnapping a child who is still missing. The suspect has been indicted and is in jail, waiting for trial. A newspaper reporter, Brian Collins, contacts Sanitation Worker Elaine Homes and asks for information that might help the reporter to investigate the kidnapping and perhaps locate the missing child. Sanitation Worker Elaine Homes should:

A. give assistance to Brian Collins by providing information that might help to locate the missing child.

B. give assistance only if the reporter can guarantee that the child will be found.

C. provide only information relating to locating the child, and not any other information.

D. not provide any information and report the request to her supervisors.

Visualization Answers 3 - 5

Answer question 3 based on the following information:

Sanitation Worker John Lagnier collects the following information at the scene of an auto accident involving a NYC Sanitation Department vehicle:

Date of Accident: August 16, 2019

Time of accident: 5:02 p.m.

Place of accident: Intersection of Ferndale Avenue and Willows Avenue, Bronx

Driver: John Lagnier (Sanitation Worker)

Vehicle: 2007 Toyota Sienna (owned by NYC Department of Sanitation)

Damage: Vehicle struck a bicycle partially parked on the sidewalk, but protruding into the street, denting the front bumper of the car.

-----

3. Sanitation Worker John Lagnier is preparing a report of the accident and has four drafts of the report. He wishes to use the draft that expresses the information most clearly, accurately and completely. Which draft should he choose?

A. At **5:20 p.m**., on August 16, 2019, at the intersection of Ferndale Avenue and Willows Avenue, Bronx, a 2007 Toyota Sienna, owned by the NYC Department of Sanitation and driven by John Lagnier (Sanitation Worker) struck a bicycle partially parked on the sidewalk, but protruding into the street.
   (**WRONG**: Time of accident is not correct. It should be **5:02** instead of **5:20**. Damage is not stated.**)**

B. At 5:02 p.m., on **August 6, 2019**, at the intersection of Ferndale Avenue and Willows Avenue, Bronx, a 2007 Toyota Sienna, owned by the NYC Department of Sanitation and driven by John Lagnier (Sanitation Worker) struck a bicycle partially parked on the sidewalk, but protruding into the street. (**WRONG:** Date is incorrect. Damage is not stated.**)**

C. At 5:02 p.m., on August 16, 2019, at the intersection of Ferndale **Street** and Willows Avenue, Bronx, a 2007 Toyota Sienna, owned by the NYC Department of Sanitation and driven by John Lagnier (Sanitation Worker) struck a bicycle partially parked on the sidewalk, but protruding into the street.
   (**WRONG:** Ferndale **Street** is wrong. It should be Ferndale **Avenue**. Damage is not stated.)

D. **At 5:02 p.m., on August 16, 2019, at the intersection of Ferndale Avenue and Willows Avenue, Bronx, a vehicle owned by the NYC Department of Sanitation and driven b**

John Lagnier (Sanitation Worker) struck a bicycle partially parked on the sidewalk, but protruding into the street, denting the front bumper of the car.

(**CORRECT.** This contains all the information and does not have any factual errors.)

Answer question 4 based on the following information:

Sanitation Worker David Larson needs to report the theft of a NYC Department of Sanitation vehicle. He has the following information:

Suspect: Unidentified

Date of crime: August 15, 2019

Time of crime: between 6:20 p.m. and 11:30 p.m.

Crime: theft of NYC Department of Sanitation auto

Vehicle stolen: 2012 Nissan

Owner of car: NYC Department of Sanitation

Place of crime: driveway in front of 167 28th Street, Staten Island

-----

4. Sanitation Worker David Larson is preparing a report of the theft and has prepared four drafts of the report. He wishes to use the draft that expresses the information most clearly, accurately and completely. Which of the following drafts should he choose?

A. On August 15, 2019, at the driveway in front of 167 28th Street, Staten Island, a 2012 Nissan owned by the NYC Department of Sanitation was stolen by an unidentified suspect.
(**WRONG.** The time of the theft is left out.)

B. On August 15, 2019, between 6:20 p.m. and 11:30 p.m., at the driveway in front of **176** 28th Street, Staten Island, a 2012 Nissan owned by the NYC Department of Sanitation was stolen by an unidentified suspect.
(**WRONG**: The place of crime address is wrong. It is stated as 176 instead of 167 28th Street, Staten Island.)

C. **On August 15, 2019, between 6:20 p.m. and 11:30 p.m., at the driveway in front of 167 28th Street, Staten Island, a 2012 Nissan owned by the NYC Department of Sanitation was stolen by an unidentified suspect.**
(**CORRECT.** This has all the information and does not contain any factual errors.)

D. On August 15, 2019, between 6:20 p.m. and 11:30 p.m., at the driveway in front of 167 28th Street, Staten Island, a Nissan owned by the NYC Department of Sanitation was stolen by an unidentified suspect.

(WRONG. The "2012" year of the Nissan is left out.**)**

Answer question 5 based on the following procedure:

Where a Sanitation Worker may be called upon to be a witness in a criminal case, the facts of which arose during the Sanitation Worker's work tour, the Sanitation Worker is prohibited from discussing the case with any newspaper, magazine, TV reporters and all other media. Exceptions to this are where:

1. a New York court of competent jurisdiction formally orders the Sanitation Worker to discuss one or more particulars of the case.
2. a NYC authorized Department orders such discussion.
3. the Sanitation Worker is subpoenaed to testify before an authorized NYC, NYS or federal board.

-----

5. Sanitation Worker Elaine Homes witnessed the kidnapping a child who is still missing. The suspect has been indicted and is in jail, waiting for trial. A newspaper reporter, Brian Collins, contacts Sanitation Worker Elaine Homes and asks for information that might help the reporter to investigate the kidnapping and perhaps locate the missing child. Sanitation Worker Elaine Homes should:

A. give assistance to Brian Collins by providing information that might help to locate the missing child.

(WRONG) This does not qualify as one of the three exception to the prohibition from discussing the case.

B. give assistance only if the reporter can guarantee that the child will be found.

(WRONG) This does not qualify as one of the three exception to the prohibition from discussing the case.

C. provide only information relating to locating the child, and not any other information.

(WRONG) This does not qualify as one of the three exception to the prohibition from discussing the case.

D. **not provide any information and report the request to her supervisors.**

(CORRECT)

PRACTICE TEST #1 QUESTIONS

Reading Comprehension

Question 1:

According to the World Health Organization, "Sanitation generally refers to the provision of facilities and services for the safe disposal of human urine and feces. Inadequate sanitation is a major cause of disease world-wide and improving sanitation is known to have a significant beneficial impact on health both in households and across communities. The word 'sanitation' also refers to the maintenance of hygienic conditions, through services such as garbage collection and wastewater disposal." *

1. Which of the following statements is best supported by the preceding paragraph?

A. The word "sanitation" refers only to the maintenance of hygienic conditions, through services such as garbage collection and wastewater disposal.

B. All Sanitation workers work in garbage collection.

C. The word "sanitation" has more than one meaning.

D. None of the above

Question 2:

The earliest evidence of urban sanitation was seen in Harappa, Mohenjo-daro and the recently discovered Rakhigarhi of Indus Valley civilization. This urban plan included the world's first urban sanitation systems. Within the city, individual homes or groups of homes obtained water from wells. From a room that appears to have been set aside for bathing, waste water was directed to covered drains, which lined the major streets.

Roman cities and Roman villas had elements of sanitation systems, delivering water in the streets of towns such as Pompeii, and building stone and wooden drains to collect and remove wastewater from populated areas. But there is little record of other sanitation in most of Europe until the High Middle Ages. Unsanitary conditions and overcrowding were widespread throughout Europe and Asia during the Middle Ages, resulting periodically in cataclysmic pandemics such as the Plague of Justinian (541-42) and the Black Death (1347–1351), which killed tens of millions of people and radically altered societies.*

2. According to the preceding passage, which of the following statements is correct?

A. Most of Europe had elements of sanitation systems before the Romans.

B. The urban plan of the recently discovered Rakhigarhi of Indus Valley civilization included the world's first urban sanitation systems.

C. The Roman sanitation system killed tens of millions of people and radically altered societies.

D. The Black Death occurred during pre-Roman times.

Questions 3:

Poor sanitation accounts for almost 50 percent of underweight children since it has a direct link to diarrhea. Children suffering for diarrhea are more vulnerable to become underweight. According to Mara, Lane, and Scott and Trouba, about 26 percent acute respiratory infections occur in children who are malnourished, which has a direct link to diarrhea. Sanitation is a serious issue that is affecting most parts of the world, especially the developing countries. On a global scale, the most affected are children who in most cases lose their lives due to diseases caused by poor sanitation. Major initiatives need to be set up if the MDG goal on sanitation is to be achieved by 2015.*

-----

3. According to the above selection, which of the following statements is correct?

A. According to Mara, Lane, and Scott and Trouba, about 26 percent of acute respiratory infections occur in adults who are malnourished.

B. Sanitation is a serious issue that is affecting most parts of the world, especially in developed countries.

C. On a global scale, most people who lose their lives due to diseases caused by poor sanitation are children.

D. Poor sanitation accounts for almost 50 percent of overweight children.

Question 4:

Disposal of solid waste is most commonly conducted in landfills, but incineration, recycling, composting and conversion to biofuels are also avenues. In the case of landfills, advanced countries typically have rigid protocols for daily cover with topsoil, where underdeveloped countries customarily rely upon less stringent protocols. The importance of daily cover lies in the reduction of vector contact and spreading of pathogens. Daily cover also minimizes odor emissions and reduces windblown litter. Likewise, developed countries typically have requirements for perimeter sealing of the landfill with clay-type soils to minimize migration of leachate that could contaminate groundwater (and hence jeopardize some drinking water supplies).*

-----

4. Which of the following statements is supported by the preceding paragraph?
A. Daily cover increases windblown litter.
B. Underdeveloped countries typically have requirements for perimeter sealing of the landfill with clay-type soils.
C. Handling of waste disposal in landfills differs among developed and underdeveloped countries.
D. Solid waste is mostly disposed of by incineration.

Question 5:

Recycling is a resource recovery practice that refers to the collection and reuse of waste materials such as empty beverage containers. The materials from which the items are made can be reprocessed into new products. Material for recycling may be collected separately from general waste using dedicated bins and collection vehicles, a procedure called curbside collection. In some communities, the owner of the waste is required to separate the materials into various different bins (e.g. for paper, plastics, metals) prior to its collection. In other communities, all recyclable materials are placed in a single bin for collection, and the sorting is handled later at a central facility. The latter method is known as "single-stream recycling." The most common consumer products recycled include aluminum such as beverage cans, copper such as wire, steel from food and aerosol cans, old steel furnishings or equipment, polyethylene and PET bottles, glass bottles and jars, paperboard cartons, newspapers, magazines and light paper, and corrugated fiberboard boxes.*

5. Which of the following statements is supported by the above paragraph?

A. One of the most common consumer products recycled is tree leaves.

B. All communities require that the consumer separate recycle materials from general waste.

C. "Single stream cycling" refers to the recycle system where the owner of the waste is required to separate the materials into various different bins (e.g. for paper, plastics, metals) prior to its collection.

D. The most common consumer products recycled include aluminum such as beverage cans, and copper such as wire.

Question 6:

A number of different systems have been implemented to collect recyclates from the general waste stream. These systems lie along the spectrum of trade-off between public convenience and government ease and expense. The three main categories of collection are "drop-off centers," "buy-back centers," and "curbside collection."

Drop-off centers require the waste producer to carry the recyclates to a central location, either an installed or mobile collection station or the reprocessing plant itself. They are the easiest type of collection to establish, but suffer from low and unpredictable supply throughput.

Buy-back centers differ in that the cleaned recyclates are purchased, thus providing a clear incentive for use and creating a stable supply. The post-processed material can then be sold on, hopefully creating a profit. Unfortunately, government subsidies are necessary to make buy-back centers a viable enterprise, as according to the United States' National Waste & Recycling Association, it costs on average $50 to process a ton of material, which can only be resold for $30.*

-----

6. Which of the following statements is supported by the above paragraph?

A. The cost to process a ton of recycle material is $30.

B. The three main categories of collection are "drop-off centers," "sell-back centers," and "curbside collection."

C. Drop-off Centers are the easiest type of collection to establish, but suffer from low and unpredictable supply throughput.

D. Recycle items are universally collected under one unified system.

Question 7 and 8:

Answer questions 7 and 8 based on the following "Human Decontamination Procedure."

Human Decontamination Procedure

Persons suspected of being contaminated are usually separated by sex, and led into a decontamination tent, trailer, or pod, where they shed their potentially contaminated clothes in a strip-down room. Then they enter a wash-down room where they are showered. Finally they enter a drying and re-robing room to be issued clean clothing, or a jumpsuit or the like. Some more structured facilities include six rooms (strip-down, wash-down and examination rooms...Facilities, such as Modecs, and many others, are remotely operable, and function like "human car washes". Mass decontamination is the decontamination of large numbers of people. The ACI World Aviation Security Standing Committee describes a decontamination process thus, specifically referring to plans for Los Angeles authorities:

The disinfection/decontamination process is akin to putting humans through a car wash after first destroying their garments. Los Angeles World Airports have put in place a contingency plan to disinfect up to 10,000 persons who might have been exposed to biological or chemical substances.*

-----

7. The above "Human Decontamination Procedure" refers to which type of decontamination?
A. only decontamination of humans exposed to biological substances.
B. only decontamination of humans exposed to chemical substances.
C. decontamination of humans exposed to chemical or biological substances.
D. none of the above

----

8. Which of the following statements is correct?
A. The Los Angeles World Airports have put in place a contingency plan to disinfect up to 1,000 persons who might have been exposed to biological or chemical substances.
B. Modecs, and many others, cannot be operated remotely.
C. Prior to persons being led to a wash-down room, they are usually separated by sex.
D. Some more structured facilities include sixty rooms.

Written Expression Questions 9-18

9. A Sanitation Worker is reviewing a report she is preparing. It contains the following two rough drafts. Which of the two sentences are grammatically correct?

   1. Man who assaulted Sanitation Worker Jeff Holmes about twenty years old and wearing blue pants and a black turtle neck sweater

   2. The man who assaulted Sanitation Worker Jeff Holmes was about twenty years old and was wearing blue pants and a black turtle neck sweater.

A. Only sentence 1 is grammatically correct.
B. Only sentence 2 is grammatically correct.
C. Both sentence 1 and 2 are grammatically correct.
D. Neither sentence 1 nor sentence 2 is grammatically correct.

----

10. A Sanitation Worker is asked by his partner to review a speech that the Sanitation Worker has volunteered to give to an eighth grade class. It contains the following two versions of one part of the speech. Which versions are grammatically correct?

   1. A reason why Sanitation Workers should know the neighborrhood is to be aware of recycling violators including their addresses.

   2. A reason Sanitation Workers should know the neighborhood they are aware of recycling violators including their addresses

A. Only sentence 1 is grammatically correct.
B. Only sentence 2 is grammatically correct.
C. Both sentence 1 and 2 are grammatically correct.
D. Neither sentence 1 nor sentence 2 is grammatically correct.

----

11. A Sanitation Worker is preparing a report and has not decided which of two versions of a specific section he wishes to use. Which of the two versions are grammatically correct?

    1. The alleged violator and his alleged accomplice has decided not to speak with the Environmental Control Officer. Both stated that they will not cooperate in any manner.

    2. Both the alleged violator and his alleged accomplice stated that they will not cooperate in any way and that they will not speak with the Environmental Control Officer.

A. Only sentence 1 is grammatically correct.
B. Only sentence 2 is grammatically correct.
C. Both sentence 1 and 2 are grammatically correct.
D. Neither sentence 1 nor sentence 2 is grammatically correct.

----

12. Sanitation Worker Charles Gates is preparing a speech that he will give at a recruiting session which his supervisor has asked him to attend. Which of the following two versions are grammatically correct?

    1. Being hired as a Sanitation Worker is not easy Sanitation Worker candidates must do well on a written test and then pass a number of other qualifying tests.

    2. Being hired as a Sanitation Worker is not easy. Sanitation Worker candidates must do well on a written test and then pass a number of other qualfying tests.

A. 1 only is correct.
B. 2 only is correct.
C. Neither 1 nor 2 is correct.
D. Both 1 and 2 are correct.

----

13. Sanitation Worker Sandra York is preparing an instruction sheet on how to respond to oral inquiries. Which of the following two sentences are correct?

    1. When responding to oral inquiries from the public, a Sanitation Worker should keep in mind that the manner in which the response is given is as important as the accuracy of the response.

    2. When a Sanitation Worker responds to oral inquiries from the public, the Sanitation Worker should keep in mind that the manner in which the response is given is as important as the accuracy of the response.

A. 1 only is correct.
B. 2 only is correct.
C. Neither 1 nor 2 is correct.
D. Both 1 and 2 are correct.

----

14. Sanitation Worker Henry Chin is checking the correctness of two versions of a section in one of his reports. Which of the following two versions are correct?

    1. Sanitation Workers wear uniforms and are required to act professionally. Because Sanitation Workers are highly visible, the impression which they create is important in establishing in the public a sense of professionalism.

    2. Because Sanitation Workers are highly visible, the impression which they create is important in establishing in the public a sense of professionalism Sanitation Workers wear uniforms and are required to act professionally.

A. 1 only is correct.   C. Neither 1 nor 2 is correct.
B. 2 only is correct.   D. Both 1 and 2 are correct.

----

15. Sanitation Worker Bryan Arber is asked to select the best summary (A, B, C or D) of the following information: (The best summary is the one that expresses the information in the most clear, accurate and complete manner.)

Place of accident: in front of 2625 North 77th Street, Jamaica
Time of accident: 10:15 P.M.
Date of accident: October 12, 2019
Vehicle involved: 2007 Armada
Driver: Sanitation Worker Helen Kierston
Damage: cracked rear headlights and cracked bumper
Details: a metal garbage container rolled into the street and struck the 2007 Armada

-----

A. On October 12, 2019, at 10:15 a.m., in front of 2625 North 77th Street., Jamaica, a metal garbage container rolled into the street and struck the 2007 Armada, driven by Sanitation Worker Helen Kierston.

B. On October 12, 2019, in front of 2625 North 77th Street., Jamaica, a metal garbage container rolled into the street and struck the 2007 Armada, driven by Sanitation Worker Helen Kierston.

C. On October 12, 2019, at 10:15 p.m., in front of 2625 North 7th Street., Jamaica, a metal garbage container rolled into the street and struck the 2007 Armada, driven by Sanitation Worker Helen Kierston.

D. On October 12, 2019, at 10:15 p.m., in front of 2625 North 77th Street., Jamaica, a metal garbage container rolled into the street and struck the 2007 Armada, driven by Sanitation Worker Helen Kierston, causing cracked rear headlights and cracked bumper.

----

16. Sanitation Worker Mohamed Bahri obtains the following information at the scene of a traffic accident:

Date of accident: November 5, 2019
Time of accident: 3:15 P.M.
Place of accident: intersection of 7th Avenue and 67th Street, New York
Vehicles involved: 2008 Nissan and 2006 Buick (owned by NYC Dept. of Sanitation)
Drivers: Benjamin Fogel (2008 Nissan) and Annette Traynor (2006 Buick)
Damage: dent on front passenger door of 2006 Buick

Sanitation Worker Mohamed Bahri drafts four versions to express the above information. Which of the following four versions is most clear, accurate and complete?

A. On November 5, 2019, at 3:15 P.M., at the intersection of 7th Avenue and 67th Street, New York, a 2008 Nissan and a 2006 Buick were involved in a traffic accident. The 2006 Buick, owned by the NYC Dept. of Sanitation and driven by Annette Traynor, sustained a dent on the passenger's front door. The 2008 Nissan, owned by Benjamin Fogel, did not sustain any damage.

B. On November 5, 2019, at 3:15 P.M., at the intersection of 7th Avenue and 67th Street, New York, a 2008 Nissan and a 2006 Buick were involved in a traffic accident. The 2008 Buick, owned by the NYC Dept. of Sanitation and driven by Annette Traynor, sustained a dent on the passenger's front door. The 2008 Nissan, driven by Benjamin Fogel, did not sustain any damage.

C. On November 5, 2019, at the intersection of 7th Avenue and 67th Street, New York, a 2008 Nissan and a 2006 Buick were involved in a traffic accident. The 2006 Buick, owned by the NYC Dept. of Sanitation and driven by Annette Traynor, sustained a dent on the passenger's front door. The 2008 Nissan, driven by Benjamin Fogel, did not sustain any damage.

D. On November 5, 2019, at 3:15 P.M., at the intersection of 7th Avenue and 67th Street, New York, a 2008 Nissan and a 2006 Buick were involved in a traffic accident. The 2006 Buick The 2008 Buick, owned by the NYC Dept. of Sanitation and driven by Annette Traynor, sustained a dent on the passenger's front door. The 2008 Nissan, driven by Benjamin Fogel, did not sustain any damage.

----

17. Which of the following words is spelled correctly?

A. beleive   C. equiptment

B. calander   D. guarantee

----

18. Which of the following four sentences does not have a grammatical error?

A. The waste collection shift has been increased by one hour most of the Sanitation Workers welcome the overtime.

B. The Sanitation Worker and her supervisor walks very quickly.

C. Although he was tired, he volunteered for another shift.

D. He went to the store and picked up diet soda crackers and cheese for them to snack on.

Problem Sensitivity Questions 19 - 25

19. A NYC Environmental Control Officer has asked Sanitation Worker John Haas to be vigilant for a male with a red baseball cap, about five feet eleven inches tall and wearing a yellow T-shirt and dark pants, who has been spotted throwing hazardous medical waste in trash containers in the area.

According to the information provided by the NYC Environmental Control Officer, Sanitation Worker Haas should: (Choose the best answer.)

A. report to the NYC Environmental Control Officer all males and females on his route.

B. report to the NYC Environmental Control Officer all males and females wearing a red baseball cap.

C. report to the NYC Environmental Control Officer all persons with the height of five feet ten inches to five feet twelve inches.

D. report to the NYC Environmental Control Officer all males on the street who are wearing a red baseball cap and are about five feet eleven inches tall and are wearing a yellow T-shirt.

----

20. Sanitation Worker Harriet Woliski notices that repulsive smelling fumes are emanating from a fire in a city garbage container at the corner of a crowded street. Sanitation Worker Harriet Woliski should:

A. immediately run into a nearby store and see if they have a fire extinguisher.

B. take off her shirt and throw it on the fire.

C. warn everyone to stay clear and contact the proper authorities.

D. wait for the fire to burn itself out before checking it out.

----

21. During his daily waste collection shift, Sanitation Worker David Callahan discovers that a manhole cover in the middle of a busy street has been removed and pungent smoke is coming out of it.

Based on the preceding information, what is the first step that Sanitation Worker David Callahan should take?

A. Call for more Sanitation Workers to act as backup.

(B) Quickly warn all the persons and traffic near the manhole and then notify the proper authorities.

C. Look for the manhole cover as it may be nearby.

D. Call the highway department and complain.

----

22. Your supervisor asks you to speak with a Mr. Jeffrey Fredrich regarding a complaint that a neighbor is continually leaving his dog unleashed and free to roam and pollute Ms. Fredrich's sidewalk and front yard. You have knowledge that there is a Mr. Jeffrey Fredrich, Sr. and a Mr. Jeffrey Fredrich, Jr. because they are the owners of a coffee shop where you are a customer. What is the first step you should take in this situation?

A. At the Fredrich home, speak with both Jeffrey Fredrich, Senior and Jeffrey Fredrich, Jr. as they have the same name.

(B) Ask your supervisor for clarification of the name of the person to speak with.

C. Disregard the supervisor's instructions because you know both Fredrich's and they are not trustworthy people.

D. Do not ask questions of your supervisor, as he might get upset.

----

23. Sanitation Worker Lorna Pearlman is on duty when a shop owner runs out of his store with his hands on his head, trying to stem a serious bleeding wound. The man yells out that he was robbed a minute ago and that the robbers sped away in a car.

Based on the preceding information, what should Sanitation Worker Pearlman do first?

A. Take the man back into the liquor store and question him regarding the robbery.

B. Interview all nearby persons to determine to see if any of them witnessed the robbery.

(C) Apply first aid to the shop owner to stop the bleeding and call for medical assistance and police.

D. Sanitation Worker Pearlman should get into her waste collection truck and attempt to catch up to the robbers.

----

24. Prior to the start of your waste collection tour, your supervisor gives you the name and address of an elderly female who reported that her metal garbage cans are being "dented" by Sanitation Workers. He asks that you speak with her regarding the advisability of switching to plastic containers. From prior experiences, you know that this person is prone to hallucinations. What is the first step you should take?

A. Carry out the instructions of your supervisor.

B. Don't speak with this person, as this would be a waste of time.

C. Prepare a report that includes that the woman is prone to hallucinations and that because of that there was no need to speak with her.

D. Check with her relatives to see if she has been hallucinating recently.

----

25. Your supervisor informs you that you and your partner will have to use Truck #24 for your waste pickup shift. It is the same truck that you turned in to the repair department the day before because it was making a "grinding noise" when driven and stopping suddenly and repeatedly (and dangerously). Your supervisor tells you that he was informed by the repair department that the problem has been fixed and that there are no other trucks available. Later, as you are driving out of the garage, you hear the same grinding noise before the truck stops suddenly. Your experienced partner suggests you keep on driving. What is the best course for you to follow?

A. Follow the advice of your partner as he is more experienced than you.

B. Stop the truck and go home, as the situation is dangerous.

C. Try to repair the truck yourself, as the repair department is obviously incompetent.

D. Inform your supervisor immediately so that he may try to resolve the problem.

_____

Deductive Reasoning Questions 26 - 28

Answer question 26 - 28 based on the information provided in the following "Waste Collection" article:

Waste Collection

Waste collection is a part of the process of waste management. It is the transfer of solid waste from the point of use and disposal to the point of treatment or landfill. Waste collection also includes the curbside collection of recyclable materials that technically are not waste, as part of a municipal landfill diversion program.

Household waste in economically developed countries will generally be left in waste containers or recycling bins prior to collection by a waste collector using a waste collection vehicle. However, in many developing countries, such as Mexico and Egypt, waste left in bins or bags at the side of the road will not be removed unless residents interact with the waste collectors. Mexico City residents must haul their trash to a waste collection vehicle which makes frequent stops around each neighborhood. The waste collectors will indicate their readiness by ringing a distinctive bell and possibly shouting. Residents line up and hand their trash container to the waste collector. A tip may be expected in some neighborhoods. Private contractor waste collectors may circulate in the same neighborhoods as many as five times per day, pushing a cart with a waste container, ringing a bell and shouting to announce their presence. These private contractors are not paid a salary and survive only on the tips they receive. Later, they meet up with a waste collection vehicle to deposit their accumulated waste.

The waste collection vehicle will often take the waste to a transfer station where it will be loaded up into a larger vehicle and sent to either a landfill or alternative waste treatment facility.*

-----

26. Which one of the following statements is supported by the preceding passage?

A. In all places in the world, waste is left in bins and is automatically picked up by waste
   collectors.

B. The term "waste collection" does not include the pick-up of recyclable materials because
   "recyclable materials" are not considered waste.

C. In Mexico City trash is picked up at curbside in front of residences.

D. In Mexico, people sometimes are expected to tip the waste collectors.

----

27. According to the preceding passage, which of the following statements is not correct?

A. In Mexico, waste collection vehicle will often take the waste to a transfer station.

B. Household waste in economically developed countries will generally be left in waste containers or recycling bins prior to collection by a waste collector using a waste collection vehicle.

C. Waste collection also includes the curbside collection of recyclable materials.

D. In many developing countries, such as Mexico and Egypt, waste left in bins or bags at the side of the road will be removed, and the residents do not need to interact with the waste collectors.

----

28. According to the preceding passage, which of the following statements is correct?

A. Waste collection is the transfer of solid and liquid waste from the point of use and disposal to the point of treatment or landfill.

B. Waste collection does not include the curbside collection of recyclable materials that technically are not waste, as part of a municipal landfill diversion program.

C. In Mexico City, waste collectors will indicate their readiness by ringing a distinctive bell and possibly shouting.

D. Household waste in economically underdeveloped countries will generally be left in waste containers or recycling bins prior to collection by a waste collector using a waste collection vehicle.

_____

Deductive Reasoning Questions 29 - 32

Answer question 29 - 32 based on the information provided in the following "Biohazard Levels" passage.

Biohazard Levels

The United States Centers for Disease Control and Prevention (CDC) categorizes various diseases in levels of biohazard, Level 1 being minimum risk and Level 4 being extreme risk.

Biohazard Level 1:

Bacteria and viruses including Bacillus subtilis, canine hepatitis, Escherichia coli, varicella (chicken pox), as well as some cell cultures and non-infectious bacteria. At this level precautions against the biohazardous materials in question are minimal, most likely involving gloves and some sort of facial protection.

Biohazard Level 2:
Bacteria and viruses that cause only mild disease to humans or are difficult to contract via aerosol in a lab setting, such as hepatitis A, B, and C, influenza A, Lyme disease, salmonella, mumps, measles, scrapie, dengue fever.
Biohazard Level 3:
Bacteria and viruses that can cause severe to fatal disease in humans, but for which vaccines or other treatments exist, such as anthrax, West Nile virus, Venezuelan equine encephalitis, SARS virus, tuberculosis, typhus, Rift Valley fever, HIV, Rocky Mountain spotted fever, yellow fever, and malaria. Among parasites Plasmodium falciparum, which causes Malaria, and Trypanosoma cruzi, which causes trypanosomiasis, also come under this level.
Biohazard Level 4:
Viruses and bacteria that cause severe to fatal disease in humans, and for which vaccines or other treatments are not available, such as Bolivian and Argentine hemorrhagic fevers, Marburg virus, Ebola virus, hantaviruses, Lassa fever virus, Crimean–Congo hemorrhagic fever, and other hemorrhagic diseases. Variola virus (smallpox) is an agent that is worked with at BSL-4 despite the existence of a vaccine. When dealing with biological hazards at this level the use of a positive pressure personnel suit, with a segregated air supply, is mandatory.*

-----

29. According to the preceding "Biohazard Levels" passage, the highest and most dangerous biohazard risk is designated as:

A. Biohazard Level 1   C. Biohazard Level 3
B. Biohazard Level 2   D. Biohazard Level 4

----

30. A "positive pressure personnel suit" must be used when dealing with Biohazard Level(s):

A. Biohazard Level 1 only   C. Biohazard Level 1, 2, 3 and 4
B. Biohazard Levels 1 and 2 only   D. Biohazard Level 4

----

31. The parasite Plasmodium falciparum, which causes Malaria Malria, comes under Biohazard Level:

A. 1   C. 3
B. 2   D. 4

----

32. Biohazardous materials most likely involving gloves and some sort of facial protection are used most likely when the biohazard level is below level:

A. 2   C. 4
B. 3   D. 5

Questions 33 – 36 are based on the following map. In answering the questions, follow the flow of traffic as indicated by the arrows. Names of streets, buildings, public areas, and points are indicated on the map.

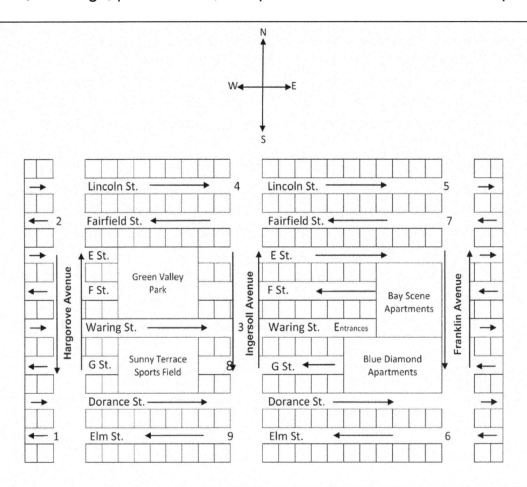

33. Imagine that you are at Hargrove Avenue and Lincoln Street and then drive East to Franklin Avenue, then drive South to Elm St., then travel West to Ingersoll Avenue, you will be closest to which one of the following points?

A. 2   B. 4   C. 5   D. 9

34. If you start your drive at point number 7, then drive West to Ingersoll Avenue, then drive South to Dorance St., then East to Franklin Avenue, then drive South to Elm St., you will be closest to which one of the following point?

A. 1   B. 5   C. 6   D. 9

35. You are in your sanitation truck at the intersection of Lincoln St. and Franklin Avenue. You are informed that you are needed at the intersection of Waring Street and Ingersoll Avenue. Assuming that you must obey all traffic rules, which one of the following four choices describes the most direct route?

A. Drive South on Franklin Avenue to Fairfield St, then drive East on Fairfield St. to Ingersoll Avenue, then South to the intersection of Waring Street and Ingersoll Avenue.

B. Drive South on Franklin Avenue to Fairfield St, then drive West on Fairfield St. to Ingersoll Avenue, then North to the intersection of Waring Street and Ingersoll Avenue.

C. Drive North on Franklin Avenue to Fairfield St, then drive East on Fairfield St. to Ingersoll Avenue, then North to the intersection of Waring Street and Ingersoll Avenue.

D. Drive South on Franklin Avenue to Fairfield St, then drive West on Fairfield St. to Ingersoll Avenue, then South to the intersection of Waring Street and Ingersoll Avenue.

----

36. You are in your sanitation truck at Hargrove Avenue and E St. You are informed that you are needed at the corner of Lincoln St. and Ingersoll Avenue. Which one of the following four choices describes the most direct route?

A. Drive South to Lincoln St. then West on Lincoln St. to the corner of Lincoln St. and Ingersoll Avenue.

B. Drive North to Lincoln St. then East on Lincoln St. to the corner of Lincoln St. and Ingersoll Avenue.

C. Drive South to Dorance St. then East on Dorance St. to Ingersoll Avenue, then North to Lincoln Street. Avenue.

D. Drive North to Lincoln St. then West on Lincoln St. to the corner of Lincoln St. and Ingersoll Avenue.

Spatial Orientation Questions 37 – 42

37. While on waste collection, you and another Sanitation Worker are stopped by an elderly woman who tells you that a "tall man" just threw hazardous medical waste on the sidewalk. You notice a "tall man" calmly walking down the block southbound to the end of the block where he makes a right turn, then observe the man continuing to walk for two blocks before making another right turn.

According to the information in the preceding passage, you would be most correct to inform your supervisor that you last saw the man walking:

A) North

B) South

C) East

D) West

----

38. While in your waste collection vehicle, you notice a car sideswipe a parked car and then drive off northbound without stopping. After four blocks the car makes a right turn and then after two more blocks makes a left turn.

According to the information in the preceding passage, you would be most correct to inform your supervisor that you last saw the car heading:

A) North

B) South

C) East

D) West

----

39. A jewelry store employee runs out of a jewelry store, points down the block and shouts, "That guy just robbed me!" The man continues running westbound. After three blocks, he make a left turn and runs for two more blocks before making another left turn.

According to the information in the preceding passage, you would be most correct to say to the police that you last saw the suspect heading:

A) North

B) South

C) East

D) West

----

40. You and another sanitation worker witness a private sanitation truck leak noxious liquids on the street. You notice that the private sanitation truck is heading in a westbound direction. You also see that it stays in that direction for three blocks before turning left and then after another block, turns right. According to the information in the preceding passage, you would be most correct to radio that the private sanitation truck is travelling:

A) North

B) South

C) East

D) West

----

41. While in your waste collection vehicle, you witness two men come out of a bar and overturn city owned trash cans, spilling the contents, including broken glass, on the sidewalk. They quickly get into a car and head northbound. After three blocks, they make a right turn and then after two more blocks they make another right turn.

According to the information in the preceding passage, you would be most correct to radio that you last saw the car heading:

A) North

B) South

C) East

D) West

----

42. Your attention is drawn to a pedestrian shouting, "He took my bike!" and pointing to a man on a bike pedaling quickly on the sidewalk, away from the pedestrian and in an westbound direction. After three blocks, he make a right turn and then after two more blocks he makes a left turn.

According to the information in the preceding passage, you would be most correct to tell the police that you last saw the man heading:

A) North

B) South

C) East

D) West

Visualization Question 43

Line
of
crates

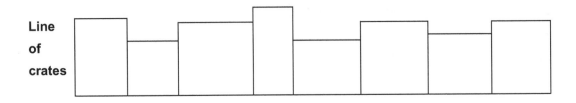

A.

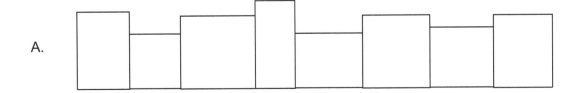

B.

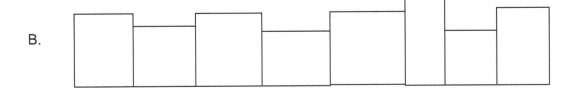

C.

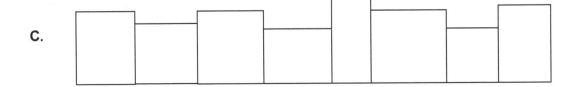

D.

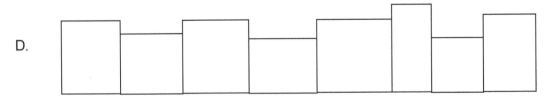

43. The above "Line of Crates" when viewed from the back would appear as which of the following choices?

A. Choice A

B. Choice B

C. Choice C

D. Choice D

Visualization Question 44

Which of the following circles (A, B, C, D) matches the image "Dissected Circle?"

A. Image A   C. Image C

B. Image B   D. Image D

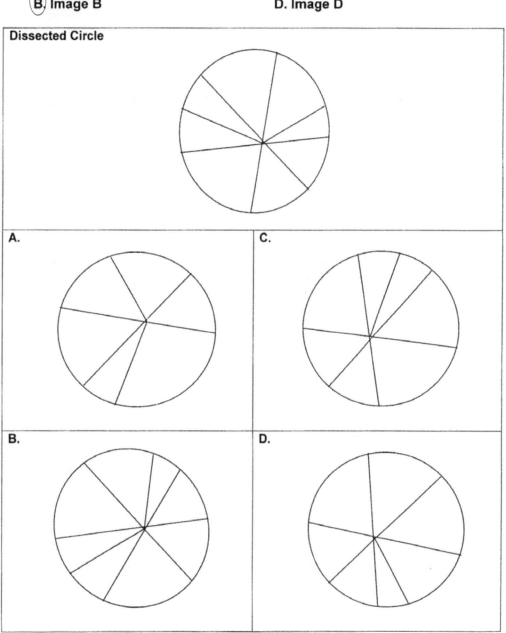

Visualization Question 45

While driving a NYC Sanitation Department vehicle, Sanitation Worker Abe Jenner is involved in an auto accident. He states that while he was driving on Vine St. in car #3, car #1 hit his rear bumper, causing him to hit vehicle number 2.

Assume that all 3 vehicles were in their proper lanes of traffic.

Which of the following 4 diagrams below best matches the statement of Sanitation Worker Abe Jenner?

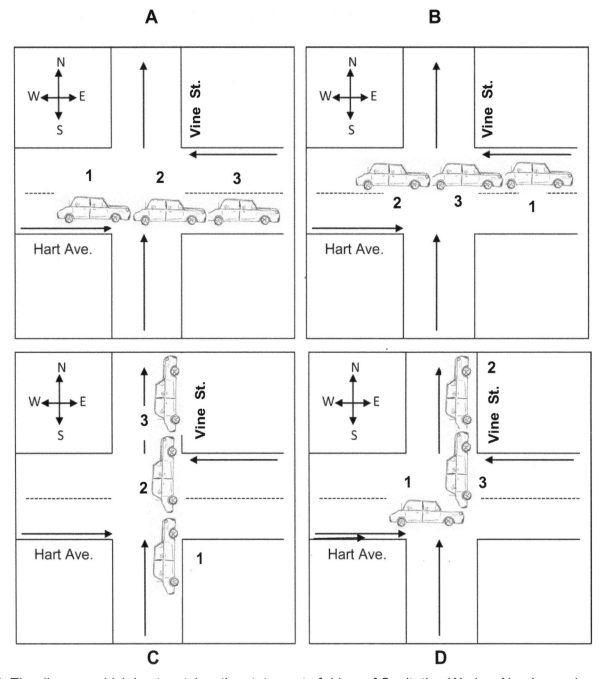

44. The diagram which best matches the statement of driver of Sanitation Worker Abe Jenner is:

A. diagram "A"

B. diagram "B"

C. diagram "C"

D. diagram "D"

Questions 46 - 47

Answer questions 46 – 47 based on the following accident details.

Sanitation Worker Dean Garullo collects the following information at the scene of an auto accident in which he was involved while driving a 2008 Toyota Sienna owned by the NYC Dept. of Sanitation.

Date of Accident: September 9, 2019
Time of accident: 4:15 p.m.
Place of accident: Intersection of Lavin Avenue and Reiker Avenue, Bronx
Driver: Sanitation Worker Dean Garullo. Owner: NYC Dept. of Sanitation
Vehicle: 2008 Toyota Sienna
Damage: Vehicle struck a commercial metal garbage container protruding into the street, causing damage to the front bumper.

-----

46. Sanitation Worker Dean Garullo is preparing a report of the accident and has four drafts of the report. He wishes to use the draft that expresses the information most clearly, accurately and completely. Which draft should he choose?

A. At 4:15 p.m., on September 9, 2019, at the intersection of Lavin Avenue and Riker Avenue, Bronx, a vehicle driven by Sanitation Worker Dean Garullo and owned by the NYC Dept. of Sanitation, struck a commercial metal garbage container protruding into the street, causing damage to the front bumper.

B. On September 7, 2019, at 4:15 p.m., at the intersection of Lavin Avenue and Reiker Avenue, Bronx, a 2008 Toyota Sienna driven by Sanitation Worker Dean Garullo and owned by the NYC Dept. of Sanitation, struck a commercial metal garbage container protruding into the street, causing damage to the front bumper.

C. On September 9, 2019, at 4:25 p.m., at the intersection of Lavin Avenue and Reiker Avenue, Bronx, a 2008 Toyota Sienna driven by Sanitation Worker Dean Garullo and owned by the NYC Dept. of Sanitation, struck a commercial metal garbage container protruding into the street, causing damage to the front bumper.

D. On September 9, 2019, at 4:15 p.m., at the intersection of Lavin Avenue and Reiker Avenue, Bronx, a 2008 Toyota Sienna driven by Sanitation Worker Dean Garullo and owned by the NYC Dept. of Sanitation, struck a commercial metal garbage container protruding into the street, causing damage to the front bumper.

47. Sanitation Worker Dean Garullo is comparing the information he recorded in his memo pad (at the scene of the accident) to the information in his report. Which of the above choices (A, B, C or D) has one detail that does not agree with the information in the Sanitation Worker's memo pad?

A. Date of Accident: September 9, 2019; Time of accident: 4:15 p.m.

B. Place of accident: Intersection of Lavin Avenue and Reiker Avenue, Bronx

C. Driver: Dean Garullo: Vehicle: 2008 Toyota Sienna

D Damage: Vehicle struck a metal commercial garbage container protruding into the street, causing

damage to the front bumper.

Answer questions 48 and 49 based on the following information gathered at a crime scene.

Sanitation Worker Henrietta Ferguson discovers that her official NYC Sanitation Department vehicle has been stolen. She gathers the following information:

Suspect: Unidentified

Date of crime: August 25, 2019

Time of crime: between 7:20 p.m. and 11:40 p.m.

Crime: theft of car

Vehicle stolen: 2012 Volvo

Owner: NYC Department of Sanitation

Driver: Sanitation Worker Henrietta Ferguson

Place of crime: driveway in front of 247 18th Street, Staten Island

-----

48. Sanitation Worker Henrietta Ferguson is preparing a report of the accident and has prepared four drafts of the report. She wishes to use the draft that expresses the information most clearly, accurately and completely. Which of the following drafts should she choose?

A. A car theft of a 2012 Volvo happened at the driveway in front of 247 18th Street, Staten Island, Staten Island where the NYC Department of Sanitation vehicle was parked. The alleged thief is unidentified, as the theft happened in the evening hours.

B. On August 25, 2019, between 7:20 p.m. and 11:40 p.m., at the driveway in front of 247 18th Street, Staten Island, a 2012 Volvo owned by the NYC Department of Sanitation and driven by Sanitation Worker Henrietta Ferguson, was stolen by an unidentified suspect.

C. A car was stolen on August 25, 2019, between 7:20 p.m. and 11:40 p.m., at the driveway in front of 247 18th Street, Staten Island, owned by Dept. of Sanitation. The suspect is unidentified.

D. On August 125 2019, 247 18th Street, Staten Island, between 7:20 a.m. and 11:40 a.m., a 2012 Volvo owned by the NYC Dept. of Sanitation was stolen by an unidentified suspect.

----

49. Sanitation Worker Henrietta Ferguson is comparing the information she recorded in her memo pad (at the scene of the crime) to the information in her report. Which of the above choices (A, B, C or D) has one detail that does not agree with the information in the Sanitation Worker's memo pad?

A. Date of crime: August 25, 2019; Time of crime: between 7:20 p.m. and 11:40 p.m.

B. Crime: theft of car; Vehicle stolen: 2012 Volvo

C. Victim: owner of car: NYC Department of Sanitation; Driver: Sanitation Worker Henrietta Ferguson

D. Place of crime: driveway in front of 247 18th Avenue, Staten Island

----

Answer question 50 - 51 based on the following "Media Inquiry Procedure."

Media Inquiry Procedure

When a criminal case is pending in the courts, a Sanitation Worker who may be called to be a witness is prohibited from discussing the case with any newspaper, magazine, TV reporters and all other media. Exceptions to this are cases where:

1. a New York court of competent jurisdiction formally orders the Sanitation Worker to discuss one or more particulars of the case.

2. a NYPD authorized Department orders such discussion

3. the Sanitation Worker is subpoenaed to testify by an authorized NYC, NYS or federal board. Media inquiries made to the Sanitation Officer should be referred to HQ Media Services at One Police Plaza.

-----

50. Sanitation Worker June Halister discovers 80 pounds of heroin in a garbage dumpster. A suspect is found, indicted, and now is in jail, waiting for trial. A newspaper reporter, Abigail Briggs, contacts Sanitation Worker June Halister and asks a quick question, the answer to which might help the reporter to investigate drug trafficking in the city. Sanitation Worker June Halister should:

A. answer the question since it is a quick question.

B. tell the reporter to contact her supervisor.

C. answer the question only if the reporter is trustworthy.

D. tell the reporter to contact HQ Media Services at One Police Plaza.

----

51. Sanitation Worker June Halister is subpoenaed to testify by an authorized federal board regarding the 80 pounds of heroin that she discovered. Based on the above, "Media Inquiry Procedure," Sanitation Worker June Halister should:

A. disregard the subpoena as it is from a federal board and she is a NYC employee.

B. call the reporter an inform her of the subpoena.

C. call in sick on the day of the subpoena in order to not testify, as per "Media Inquiry Procedure."

D. Inform her supervisor and obey the subpoena.

Information Ordering Questions 52 - 54

If a waste collection truck breaks down, the Sanitation Worker assigned to drive the truck should first notify the local headquarters. The driver should relay the truck ID number, the location of the truck, and the suspected problem with the truck. Neither the driver nor his partner on the assignment should attempt to fix the truck. Both the driver and his partner should remain with the truck and be present when the repair detail comes to repair the truck. As soon as the truck is repaired, the driver should notify the local headquarters. He should also notify the local headquarters when garbage pickup resumes. The driver, either at the scene or upon the return to the garage, must enter all the pertinent information in the truck's daily journal.

Based on the preceding procedures, after relaying to headquarters the truck ID number, the location of the truck, and the suspected problem with the truck described above, the next thing the driver or his partner should do is:

A. relay to headquarters the names of the repair crew.

B. attempt to fix the truck

C. notify local headquarters of the vehicle break-down.

D. remain with the truck.

53. The sanitation worker working with the driver must enter all the pertinent information in the truck's daily journal:

A. only at the scene

B. only upon return to the garage

C. at the scene or upon the return to the garage

D. none of the above

54. After the truck is repaired, what is the next step that should be taken?

A. resume the garbage collection route.

B. take the truck on at least a ten minute drive to evaluate its performance.

C. the driver should notify the local headquarters.

D. none of the above

Information Ordering Questions 55 - 57

The following five sentences (listed in random order) are the five necessary steps to properly record and process a Sanitation Worker's pre-approved overtime. Which one of the following choices (A, B, C, D) lists the order of sentences which best expresses the logical sequence of the proper recording and processing of pre-approved overtime?

1. A the end of the bi-weekly pay period, record the Overtime Worked Report Confirmation Number in section 2 of the Bi-Weekly Pay Period Report.

2. Sign the Bi-Weekly Pay Period Report and submit it to the Local Sanitation Station.

3. After the approved overtime work shift, submit to the local Sanitation Station a completed "Overtime Worked Report" and obtain an Overtime Worked Report Confirmation Number for its submission.

4. Obtain pre-approval from the local Sanitation Station.

5. Work the number of overtime hours requested on the approved overtime pre-approval form.

55. Which of the following choices lists the most logical sequence of steps for the proper recording and processing of pre-approved overtime?

A. 5, 1 ,3 ,2, 4

B. 4, 5, 3, 1, 2

C. 5, 1, 4, 3, 2

D. 5, 4, 1, 3, 2

56. According to the above steps for the proper recording and processing of pre-approved overtime, the periodic Pay Period Report must be submitted to the Local Sanitation Station:

A. every day

B. every week

C. every month

D. none of the above

57. According to the above steps for the recording and processing of pre-approved overtime, which of the following statements is not correct?

A. Pre-approval for the overtime is obtained from the local Sanitation Station.

B. The Bi-Weekly Pay Period Report is signed by the Sanitation Worker.

C. The pay-period is bi-weekly.

D. An Overtime Worked Report Confirmation Number must be obtained prior to working overtime.

Information Ordering Questions 58 - 60

The following are four sentences. Each sentence (listed in random order) is one of the four steps necessary to sign-out a snow plow at the Sanitation Department garage at the beginning of a shift.

1. Locate the assigned snow plow and visually inspect it for any obvious defects or missing equipment.

2. Drive slowly out of the garage to make sure that the Snow Plow is in good operational order and does not have mechanical defects..

3. Sign the "Snow Plow Assignment Log" at the Superintendent's office and obtain the keys to the Snow Plow."

4. Obtain from the garage superintendent the ID number of the snow plow assigned to you.

58. Which one of the following choices (A, B, C, D) lists the order of sentences which best expresses the logical sequence of signing-out for a snow plow?

A. 1, 4, 2, 3

B. 2, 3, 4, 1

C. 4, 1, 3, 2

D. 3, 4, 2, 1

59. According to the above Snow Plow Sign-Out procedure, the snow plow should be inspected for mechanical defects:

A. in the morning.

B. in the afternoon.

C. in the evening.

D. none of the above

60 According to the above procedure, which of the following is not correct?

A. The License plate number of the snow plow assigned to you is obtained from the garage superintendent.

B. The "Snow Plow Assignment Log" is signed by the driver.

C. Drive slowly out of the garage to make sure that the Snow Plow is in good operational order and does not have mechanical defects.

D. Locate the assigned snow plow and visually inspect it for any obvious defects or missing equipment.

END of Practice Test 1

PRACTICE TEST #1 ANSWERS

Reading Comprehension

Question 1 Answer:

According to the World Health Organization, "Sanitation generally refers to the provision of facilities and services for the safe disposal of human urine and feces. Inadequate sanitation is a major cause of disease world-wide and improving sanitation is known to have a significant beneficial impact on health both in households and across communities. The word 'sanitation' also refers to the maintenance of hygienic conditions, through services such as garbage collection and wastewater disposal." *

1. Which of the following statements is best supported by the preceding paragraph?

A. The word "sanitation" refers only to the maintenance of hygienic conditions, through services such as garbage collection and wastewater disposal.

   (NOT CORRECT). According to the paragraph, the word "sanitation" refers to more than one meaning.

B. All Sanitation workers work in garbage collection.

   (NOT CORRECT) Sanitation workers who collect garbage perform only one aspect of the work referred to by the word "sanitation."

C. The word "sanitation" has more than one meaning.

   (CORRECT. THIS IS THE ANSWER. "The word 'sanitation' also refers to the maintenance of hygienic conditions, through services such as garbage collection and wastewater disposal.")

D. None of the above

   (NOT CORRECT. Choice "C" is a true statement that is supported by the paragraph.)

Question 2 Answer:

The earliest evidence of urban sanitation was seen in Harappa, Mohenjo-daro and the recently discovered Rakhigarhi of Indus Valley civilization. This urban plan included the world's first urban sanitation systems. Within the city, individual homes or groups of homes obtained water from wells. From a room that appears to have been set aside for bathing, waste water was directed to covered drains, which lined the major streets.

Roman cities and Roman villas had elements of sanitation systems, delivering water in the streets of towns such as Pompeii, and building stone and wooden drains to collect and remove wastewater from populated areas. But there is little record of other sanitation in most of Europe until the High Middle Ages. Unsanitary conditions and overcrowding were widespread throughout Europe and Asia during the Middle Ages, resulting periodically in cataclysmic pandemics such as the Plague of Justinian (541-42) and the Black Death (1347–1351), which killed tens of millions of people and radically altered societies.*

-----

2. According to the preceding passage, which of the following statements is correct?

A. Most of Europe had elements of sanitation systems before the Romans.

   (**NOT CORRECT.** The reverse is true.)

B. **The urban plan of the recently discovered Rakhigarhi of Indus Valley civilization included the world's first urban sanitation systems.**

   (**This statement is CORRECT. "B" is the answer.** "The earliest evidence of urban sanitation was seen in Harappa, Mohenjo-daro and the recently discovered Rakhigarhi of Indus Valley civilization. This urban plan included the world's first urban sanitation systems.")

C. The Roman sanitation system killed tens of millions of people and radically altered societies.

   (**NOT CORRECT.** "Unsanitary conditions and overcrowding were widespread throughout Europe and Asia during the Middle Ages, resulting periodically in cataclysmic pandemics...which killed tens of millions of people and radically altered societies.")

D. The Black Death occurred during pre-Roman times.

   (**NOT CORRECT.** The Black Death occurred during the Middle Ages, after the time of the Romans.)

Questions 3 Answer:

Poor sanitation accounts for almost 50 percent of underweight children since it has a direct link to diarrhea. Children suffering for diarrhea are more vulnerable to become underweight. According to Mara, Lane, and Scott and Trouba, about 26 percent acute respiratory infections occur in children who are malnourished, which has a direct link to diarrhea. Sanitation is a serious issue that is affecting most parts of the world, especially the developing countries. On a global scale, the most affected are children who in most cases lose their lives due to diseases caused by poor sanitation. Major initiatives need to be set up if the MDG goal on sanitation is to be achieved by 2015.*

-----

3. According to the above selection, which of the following statements is correct?

A. According to Mara, Lane, and Scott and Trouba, about 26 percent of acute respiratory infections occur in adults who are malnourished.

   (**NOT CORRECT.** "...about 26 percent of acute respiratory infections occur in children who are malnourished.")

B. Sanitation is a serious issue that is affecting most parts of the world, especially in developed countries.

(**NOT CORRECT.** "Sanitation is a serious issue that is affecting most parts of the world, especially the <u>developing</u> countries.")

C. <u>**On a global scale, most people who lose their lives due to diseases caused by poor sanitation are children**</u>.

(**CORRECT. THIS IS THE ANSWER.** "On a global scale, the most affected are children who in most cases lose their lives due to diseases caused by poor sanitation.")

D. Poor sanitation accounts for almost 50 percent of overweight children.

(**NOT CORRECT.** "Poor sanitation accounts for almost 50 percent of <u>underweight</u> children.)

Question 4 Answer:

Disposal of solid waste is most commonly conducted in landfills, but incineration, recycling, composting and conversion to biofuels are also avenues. In the case of landfills, <u>advanced countries typically have rigid protocols for daily cover with topsoil, where underdeveloped countries customarily rely upon less stringent protocols</u>. The importance of daily cover lies in the reduction of vector contact and spreading of pathogens. Daily cover also minimizes odor emissions and reduces windblown litter. Likewise, developed countries typically have requirements for perimeter sealing of the landfill with clay-type soils to minimize migration of leachate that could contaminate groundwater (and hence jeopardize some drinking water supplies).*

-----

4. Which of the following statements is supported by the preceding paragraph?

A. Daily cover increases windblown litter.

(**NOT CORRECT.** "Daily cover also minimizes odor emissions and <u>reduces</u> windblown litter.")

B. Underdeveloped countries typically have requirements for perimeter sealing of the landfill with clay-type soils.

(**NOT CORRECT.** "<u>Developed</u> countries typically have requirements for perimeter sealing of the landfill with clay-type soils.")

C. <u>**Handling of waste disposal in landfills differs among developed and underdeveloped countries**</u>.

(**CORRECT. THIS IS THE ANSWER.** This is the main point of the paragraph.)

D. Solid waste is mostly disposed of by incineration.

(**NOT CORRECT.** "Disposal of solid waste is most commonly conducted in landfills.")

Question 5 Answer:

Recycling is a resource recovery practice that refers to the collection and reuse of waste materials such as empty beverage containers. The materials from which the items are made can be reprocessed into new products. Material for recycling <u>may be collected separately</u> from general waste using dedicated bins and collection vehicles, a procedure called curbside collection. In some communities, the owner of the waste is required to separate the materials into various different bins (e.g. for paper, plastics, metals) prior to its collection. In other communities, all recyclable materials are placed in a single bin for collection, and the sorting is handled later at a central facility. The latter method is known as "single-stream recycling."

<u>The most common consumer products recycled include aluminum such as beverage cans, copper such as wire, steel from food and aerosol cans, old steel furnishings or equipment, polyethylene and PET bottles, glass bottles and jars, paperboard cartons, newspapers, magazines and light paper, and corrugated fiberboard boxes.</u>*

-----

5. Which of the following statements is supported by the above paragraph?

A. One of the most common consumer products recycled is tree leaves.

   (**NOT CORRECT**. Tree leaves are not mentioned in the paragraph. Also, they are not a "consumer product" that is manufactured.)

B. All communities require that the consumer separate recycle materials from general waste.

   (**NOT CORRECT**. "Material for recycling <u>may</u> be collected separately from general waste.")

C. "Single stream cycling" refers to the recycle system where the owner of the waste is required to separate the materials into various different bins (e.g. for paper, plastics, metals) prior to its collection.

   (**NOT CORRECT**. "Single stream recycling" refers to a recycling system where all recyclable materials are placed in a <u>single bin</u> for collection, and the sorting is handled later at a central facility.)

D. The most common consumer products recycled include aluminum such as beverage cans, and copper such as wire.

   (**CORRECT. THIS IS THE ANSWER.** "The most common consumer products recycled include aluminum such as beverage cans, copper such as wire, steel from food and aerosol cans, old steel furnishings or equipment, polyethylene and PET bottles, glass bottles and jars, paperboard cartons, newspapers, magazines and light paper, and corrugated fiberboard boxes.")

Question 6 Answer:

<u>A number of different systems</u> have been implemented to collect recyclates from the general waste stream. These systems lie along the spectrum of trade-off between public convenience and government ease and expense. The three main categories of collection are <u>"drop-off centers," "buy-back centers," and "curbside collection"</u>.

<u>Drop-off centers</u> require the waste producer to carry the recyclates to a central location, either an installed or mobile collection station or the reprocessing plant itself. <u>They are the easiest type of collection to establish, but suffer from low and unpredictable supply throughput</u>.

Buy-back centers differ in that the cleaned recyclates are purchased, thus providing a clear incentive for use and creating a stable supply. The post-processed material can then be sold on, hopefully creating a profit. Unfortunately, government subsidies are necessary to make buy-back centers a viable enterprise, as according to the United States' National Waste & Recycling Association, it costs on average <u>$50 to process a ton of material,</u> which can only be resold for $30.*

-----

6. Which of the following statements is supported by the above paragraph?

A. The cost to process a ton of recycle material is $30.

   (**NOT CORRECT**. ("...it costs on average **$50** to process a ton of material, which can only be resold for $30.")

B. The three main categories of collection are "drop-off centers," "sell-back centers," and "curbside collection.")

   (**NOT CORRECT**. "The three main categories of collection are "drop-off centers," "<u>buy</u>-back centers," and "curbside collection.")

C. Drop-off Centers are the easiest type of collection to establish, but suffer from low and unpredictable supply throughput.

   (**CORRECT. THIS IS THE ANSWER.** "Drop-off centers require the waste producer to carry the recyclates to a central location, either an installed or mobile collection station or the reprocessing plant itself. They are the easiest type of collection to establish, but suffer from low and unpredictable supply throughput.")

D. Recycle items are universally collected under one unified system.

   (**NOT CORRECT**. "A number of different systems have been implemented to collect recyclates from the general waste stream.")

Question 7 and 8 Answers:

Answer questions 7 and 8 based on the following "Human Decontamination Procedure."

Human Decontamination Procedure

<u>Persons suspected of being contaminated are usually separated by sex</u>, and led into a decontamination tent, trailer, or pod, where they shed their potentially contaminated clothes in a strip-down room. Then they enter a wash-down room where they are showered. Finally they enter a drying and re-robing room to be issued clean clothing, or a jumpsuit or the like. Some more structured facilities include <u>six rooms</u> (strip-down, wash-down and examination rooms...Facilities, such as Modecs, and many others, are <u>remotely operable</u>, and function like "human car washes". Mass decontamination is the decontamination of large numbers of people. The ACI World Aviation Security Standing Committee describes a decontamination process thus, specifically referring to plans for Los Angeles authorities:

The disinfection/decontamination process is akin to putting humans through a car wash after first destroying their garments. Los Angeles World Airports have put in place a contingency plan to disinfect up to <u>10,000</u> persons who might have been exposed to <u>biological or chemical substances.</u>*

-----

7. The above "Human Decontamination Procedure" refers to which type of decontamination?

A. only decontamination of humans exposed to biological substances.

B. only decontamination of humans exposed to chemical substances.

C. decontamination of humans exposed to chemical or biological substances.

   (**THIS IS THE ANSWER.** "The ACI World Aviation Security Standing Committee
   describes a decontamination process thus...who might have been exposed to
   <u>biological or chemical substances</u>.")

D. none of the above

----

8. Which of the following statements is correct?

A. The Los Angeles World Airports have put in place a contingency plan to disinfect up to
   1,000 persons who might have been exposed to biological or chemical substances.
   (**NOT CORRECT**. The number of person is 10,000 and not 1,000.)

B. Modecs, and many others, cannot be operated remotely.
   NOT CORRECT. "Modecs, and many others, are remotely operable, and function like
   "human car washes.")

C. Prior to persons being led to a wash-down room, they are usually separated by sex.

   (**CORRECT.** "Persons suspected of being contaminated are usually <u>separated by
   sex,</u> and led into a decontamination tent, trailer, or pod, where they shed their
   potentially contaminated clothes in a strip-down room. Then they enter a wash-down
   room where they are showered.")

D. Some more structured facilities include sixty rooms.
   (**NOT CORRECT**. Correct number of rooms is <u>six.</u>)

Written Expression Answers 9 – 18

9. A Sanitation Worker is reviewing a report she is preparing. It contains the following two rough drafts. Which of the two sentences are grammatically correct?

1. Man who assaulted Sanitation Worker Jeff Holmes about twenty years old and wearing blue pants and a black turtle neck sweater

2. The man who assaulted Sanitation Worker Jeff Holmes was about twenty years old and was wearing blue pants and a black turtle neck sweater.

A. Only sentence 1 is grammatically correct.

B. Only sentence 2 is grammatically correct.

C. Both sentence 1 and 2 are grammatically correct.

D. Neither sentence 1 nor sentence 2 is grammatically correct.

Sentence 1 is clumsy and confusing. It is a run-on sentence and also needs a period at the end of the sentence.

----

10. A Sanitation Worker is asked by his partner to review a speech that the Sanitation Worker has volunteered to give to an eighth grade class. It contains the following two versions of one part of the speech. Which versions are grammatically correct?

1. A reason why Sanitation Workers should know the neighborrhood is to be aware of recycling violators including their addresses.

2. A reason Sanitation Workers should know the neighborhood they are aware of recycling violators including their addresses

A. Only sentence 1 is grammatically correct.

B. Only sentence 2 is grammatically correct.

C. Both sentence 1 and 2 are grammatically correct.

D. Neither sentence 1 nor sentence 2 is grammatically correct.

In version 1 "neighborhood" is misspelled "neighborrhood." A comma is also needed between "violators" and "including."

Version 2 is comprised of a sentence (They are aware of recycling violators including their addresses) and a sentence fragment (a reason Sanitation Workers should know the neighborhood) that are joined without appropriate connecting words. A period is also needed at the end of the sentence.

----

11. A Sanitation Worker is preparing a report and has not decided which of two versions of a specific section he wishes to use. Which of the two versions are grammatically correct?

1. The alleged violator and his alleged accomplice has decided not to speak with the Environmental Control Officer. Both stated that they will not cooperate in any manner.

2. Both the alleged violator and his alleged accomplice stated that they will not cooperate in any way and that they will not speak with the Environmental Control Officer.

A. Only sentence 1 is grammatically correct.

B. Only sentence 2 is grammatically correct.

C. Both sentence 1 and 2 are grammatically correct.

D. Neither sentence 1 nor sentence 2 is grammatically correct.

In sentence 1 the subject of the sentence "alleged violator and his alleged accomplice" (plural) disagrees with the verb "has" (singular)." A correct version would be:

"The alleged violator and his alleged accomplice <u>have</u> decided not to speak with the Environmental Control Officer. Both stated that they will not cooperate in any manner."

----

12. Sanitation Worker Charles Gates is preparing a speech that he will give at a recruiting session which his supervisor has asked him to attend. Which of the following two versions are grammatically correct?

1. Being hired as a Sanitation Worker is not easy Sanitation Worker candidates must do well on a written test and then pass a number of other qualifying tests.

2. Being hired as a Sanitation Worker is not easy. Sanitation Worker candidates must do well on a written test and then pass a number of other qualfying tests.

A. 1 only is correct.

B. 2 only is correct.

C. Neither 1 nor 2 is correct.

D. Both 1 and 2 are correct.

Sentence 1 is a run-on sentence. It needs to be expressed in two sentences.

Sentence 2 is not correct because the work "qualifying" is misspelled "qualfying."

----

13. Sanitation Worker Sandra York is preparing an instruction sheet on how to respond to oral inquiries. Which of the following two sentences are correct?

1. When responding to oral inquiries from the public, a Sanitation Worker should keep in mind that the manner in which the response is given is as important as the accuracy of the response.

2. When a Sanitation Worker responds to oral inquiries from the public, the Sanitation Worker should keep in mind that the manner in which the response is given is as important as the accuracy of the response.

A. 1 only is correct.
B. 2 only is correct.
C. Neither 1 nor 2 is correct.
D. Both 1 and 2 are correct.

----

14. Sanitation Worker Henry Chin is checking the correctness of two versions of a section in one of his reports. Which of the following two versions are correct?

1. Sanitation Workers wear uniforms and are required to act professionally. Because Sanitation Workers are highly visible, the impression which they create is important in establishing in the public a sense of professionalism.

2. Because Sanitation Workers are highly visible, the impression which they create is important in establishing in the public a sense of professionalism Sanitation Workers wear uniforms and are required to act professionally.

A. 1 only is correct.   C. Neither 1 nor 2 is correct.

B. 2 only is correct.   D. Both 1 and 2 are correct.

Sentence 2 is a run-on sentence. Two or more sentences are joined without proper connecting words. A correct version is "Because Sanitation Workers are highly visible, the impression which they create is important in establishing in the public a sense of professionalism. Sanitation Workers wear uniforms and are required to act professionally."

----

15. Sanitation Worker Bryan Arber is asked to select the best summary (A, B, C or D) of the following information: (The best summary is the one that expresses the information in the most clear, accurate and complete manner.)

Place of accident: in front of 2625 North 77th Street, Jamaica

Time of accident: 10:15 P.M.

Date of accident: October 12, 2019

Vehicle involved: 2007 Armada

Driver: Sanitation Worker Helen Kierston

Damage: cracked rear headlights and cracked bumper

Details: a metal garbage container rolled into the street and struck the 2007 Armada

-----

A. On October 12, 2019, at **10:15 a.m.,** in front of 2625 North 77th Street., Jamaica, a metal garbage container rolled into the street and struck the 2007 Armada, driven by Sanitation Worker Helen Kierston. **(Time is incorrect. Correct time is 10:15 P.M.)**

B. On October 12, 2019, in front of 2625 North 77th Street., Jamaica, a metal garbage container rolled into the street and struck the 2007 Armada, driven by Sanitation Worker Helen Kierston. **(The time of the accident is omitted.)**

C. On October 12, 2019, at 10:15 p.m., in front of 2625 North 7th Street., Jamaica, a metal garbage container rolled into the street and struck the 2007 Armada, driven by Sanitation Worker Helen Kierston. **(The address is wrong. Correct address is 2625 North 77th Street, Jamaica.)**

D. **On October 12, 2019, at 10:15 p.m., in front of 2625 North 77th Street., Jamaica, a metal garbage container rolled into the street and struck the 2007 Armada, driven by Sanitation Worker Helen Kierston, causing cracked rear headlights and cracked bumper.**
(Correct answer. It includes all of the information and has no factual errors.)

----

16. Sanitation Worker Mohamed Bahri obtains the following information at the scene of a traffic accident:

Date of accident: November 5, 2019

Time of accident: 3:15 P.M.

Place of accident: intersection of 7th Avenue and 67th Street, New York

Vehicles involved: 2008 Nissan and 2006 Buick (owned by NYC Dept of Sanitation)

Drivers: Benjamin Fogel (2008 Nissan) and Annette Traynor (2006 Buick)

Damage: dent on front passenger door of 2006 Buick

Sanitation Worker Mohamed Bahri drafts four versions to express the above information. Which of the following four versions is most clear, accurate and complete?

A. On November 5, 2019, at 3:15 P.M., at the intersection of 7th Avenue and 67th Street, New York, a 2008 Nissan and a 2006 Buick were involved in a traffic accident. The 2006 Buick, owned by the NYC Dept. of Sanitation, sustained a dent on the passenger's front door. The 2008 Nissan, **owned** by Benjamin Fogel, did not sustain any damage. **(Wrong because Benjamin Fogel is the <u>driver</u> of the vehicle.)**

B. On November 5, 2019, at 3:15 P.M., at the intersection of 7th Avenue and 67th Street, New York, a 2008 Nissan and a 2006 Buick were involved in a traffic accident. The **2008 Buick,** owned by the NYC Dept. of Sanitation and driven by Annette Traynor, sustained a dent on the passenger's front door. The 2008 Nissan, driven by Benjamin Fogel, did not sustain any damage.

(Wrong because the damage was sustained by the <u>2006 Buick</u>.)

C. On November 5, 2019, at the intersection of 7th Avenue and 67th Street, New York, a 2008 Nissan and a 2006 Buick were involved in a traffic accident. The 2006 Buick, owned by the NYC Dept. of Sanitation and driven by Annette Traynor, sustained a dent on the passenger's front door. The 2008 Nissan, driven by Benjamin Fogel, did not sustain any damage. **(Wrong because the time of the accident is not stated.)**

D. **On November 5, 2019, at 3:15 P.M., at the intersection of 7th Avenue and 67th Street, New York, a 2008 Nissan and a 2006 Buick were involved in a traffic accident. The 2006 Buick, owned by the NYC Dept. of Sanitation and driven by Annette Traynor, sustained a dent on the passenger's front door. The 2008 Nissan, driven by Benjamin Fogel, did not sustain any damage.**

(Correct answer. It includes all of the information and has no factual errors.)

----

17. Which of the following words is spelled correctly?
A. beleive
   (WRONG. Correct spelling is "believe.")
B. calander
   (WRONG. Correct spelling is "calendar.")
C. equiptment
   (WRONG. Correct spelling is "equipment.")
D. guarantee
   'CORRECT. THIS IS THE ANSWER.)

18. Which of the following four sentences does not have a grammatical error?

A. The waste collection shift has been increased by one hour most of the Sanitation Workers welcome the overtime.

(**NOT CORRECT**. It is a run-on sentence. A correct version would be: "The waste collection shift has been increased by one hour. Most of the Sanitation Workers welcome the overtime.")

B. The Sanitation Worker and her supervisor walks very quickly.

(**NOT CORRECT**. There is no subject/verb agreement between the subject "The Sanitation Worker and her supervisor," (plural) and the verb "walks," which is singular. A correct version would be: "The Sanitation Worker and her supervisor **walk** very quickly.")

C. Although he was tired, he volunteered for another shift.

(**CORRECT. THIS IS THE ANSWER.** It is grammatically correct.)

D. He went to the store and picked up diet soda crackers and cheese for them to snack on.

(**NOT CORRECT**. A comma is missing between "soda" and "crackers." A correct version would be: "He went to the store and picked up diet soda, crackers and cheese for them to snack on.")

Problem Sensitivity Answers 19 - 25

19. A NYC Environmental Control Officer has asked Sanitation Worker John Haas to be vigilant for a male with a red baseball cap, about five feet eleven inches tall and wearing a yellow T-shirt and dark pants, who has been spotted throwing hazardous medical waste in trash containers in the area.

According to the information provided by the NYC Environmental Control Officer, Sanitation Worker Haas should: (Choose the best answer.)

A. report to the NYC Environmental Control Officer all males and females on his route.

B. report to the NYC Environmental Control Officer all males and females wearing a red baseball cap.

C. report to the NYC Environmental Control Officer all persons with the height of five feet ten inches to five feet twelve inches.

D. report to the NYC Environmental Control Officer all males on the street who are wearing a red baseball cap and are about five feet eleven inches tall and are wearing a yellow T-shirt.

("D" is correct because reporting all persons who fit just one of the description items is not useful. The combination of a red baseball cap and the appropriate height and yellow color of the T-shirt zeroes in on possible suspects without involving innocent people.)

----

20. Sanitation Worker Harriet Woliski notices that repulsive smelling fumes are emanating from a fire in a city garbage container at the corner of a crowded street. Sanitation Worker Harriet Woliski should:

A. immediately run into a nearby store and see if they have a fire extinguisher.

B. take off her shirt and throw it on the fire.

C. warn everyone to stay clear and contact the proper authorities.

("C" is correct because the "repulsive smelling fumes" might be an indication of hazardous chemicals. This is a possible emergency situation. To protect the public and herself, everyone should be warned to stay clear. Also, the proper authorities should be contacted so they can investigate the toxicity of the fumes and also extinguish the fire.)

D. wait for the fire to burn itself out before checking it out.

----

21. During his daily collection shift, Sanitation Worker David Callahan discovers that a manhole cover in the middle of a busy street has been removed and pungent smoke is coming out of it.

Based on the preceding information, what is the first step that Sanitation Worker David Callahan should take?

A. Call for more Sanitation Workers to act as backup.

B. Quickly warn all the persons and traffic near the manhole and then notify the proper authorities.

(**"B" is correct.** This is similar to the preceding question. Because the "pungent smoke" might be an indication of hazardous chemicals, this is a possible emergency situation. To protect the public, people should be warned to stay clear. Also, the proper authorities should be contacted so they can investigate the toxicity of the fumes.)

C. Look for the manhole cover as it may be nearby.

D. Call the highway department and complain.

----

22. Your supervisor asks you to speak with a Mr. Jeffrey Fredrich regarding a complaint that a neighbor is continually leaving his dog unleashed and free to roam and pollute Mr. Fredrich's sidewalk and front yard. You have knowledge that there is a Mr. Jeffrey Fredrich, Sr. and a Mr. Jeffrey Fredrich, Jr. because they are the owners of a coffee shop where you are a customer. What is the first step you should take in this situation?

A. At the Fredrich home, speak with both Jeffrey Fredrich, Senior and Jeffrey Fredrich, Jr. as they have the same name.

B. Ask your supervisor for clarification of the name of the person to speak with.

("B" is correct because Sanitation Workers should always get clarification when they have questions about instructions given to them by their supervisors. This helps the Sanitation Workers to properly carry out the instructions and also helps to diminish unnecessary negative consequences that may result from misunderstood instructions.)

C. Disregard the supervisor's instructions because you know both Fredrich's and they are not trustworthy people.

D. Do not ask questions of your supervisor, as he might get upset.

----

23. Sanitation Worker Lorna Pearlman is on duty when a shop owner runs out of his store with his hands on his head, trying to stem a serious bleeding wound. The man yells out that he was robbed a minute ago and that the robbers sped away in a car.

Based on the preceding information, what should Sanitation Worker Pearlman do first?

A. Take the man back into the liquor store and question him regarding the robbery.

B. Interview all nearby persons to determine to see if any of them witnessed the robbery.

C. Apply first aid to the shop owner to stop the bleeding and call for medical assistance and police.

("C" is correct because bleeding wounds should be attended to first. The Sanitation Worker correctly should apply first aid, then call for further medical assistance. Once this life-threatening issue is addressed, then the Sanitation Worker should provide information to Police Officers to aid in the investigation of the alleged robbery.)

D. Sanitation Worker Pearlman should get into her waste collection truck and attempt to catch up to the robbers.

----

24. Prior to the start of your waste collection tour, your supervisor gives you the name and address of an elderly female who reported that her metal garbage cans are being "dented" by Sanitation Workers. He asks that you speak with her regarding the advisability of switching to plastic containers. From prior experiences, you know that this person is prone to hallucinations. What is the first step you should take?

A. Carry out the instructions of your supervisor.

("A" is correct because proper instructions should be carried out. If the Sanitation Worker has questions or suggestions, the Sanitation Worker should bring them to the attention of the supervisor and not modify or disregard them.)

B. Don't speak with this person, as this would be a waste of time.

C. Prepare a report that includes that the woman is prone to hallucinations and that because of that there was no need to speak with her.

D. Check with her relatives to see if she has been hallucinating recently.

----

25. Your supervisor informs you that you and your partner will have to use Truck #24 for your waste pickup shift. It is the same truck that you turned in to the repair department the day before because it was making a "grinding noise" when driven and stopping suddenly and repeatedly (and dangerously). Your supervisor tells you that he was informed by the repair department that the problem has been fixed and that there are no other trucks available. Later, as you are driving out of the garage, you hear the same grinding noise before the truck stops suddenly. Your experienced partner suggests you keep on driving. What is the best course for you to follow?

A. Follow the advice of your partner as he is more experienced than you.

(**NOT CORRECT**. Although your partner is experienced, he is wrong. If unrepaired, the mechanical problem might result in personal injury or increased damage to the vehicle.)

B. Stop the truck and go home, as the situation is dangerous.

(**NOT CORRECT.** Such dramatic action is uncalled for and may result in disciplinary action. A responsible Sanitation Worker tries to resolve problems and not run away from them.)

C. Try to repair the truck yourself, as the repair department is obviously incompetent.

(**NOT CORRECT.** The equipment should be repaired by professional **repair** people and not by a Sanitation Worker.)

D. **Inform your supervisor immediately so that he may try to resolve the problem.**

(**CORRECT. THIS IS THE BEST COURSE FOR YOU TO FOLLOW.** If unrepaired, the mechanical problem might result in personal injury or increased damage to the vehicle.)

Deductive Reasoning Answers 26 - 28

Answer question 26 - 28 based on the information provided in the following "Waste Collection" article:

Waste Collection

Waste collection is a part of the process of waste management. It is the transfer of solid waste from the point of use and disposal to the point of treatment or landfill. Waste collection also includes the curbside collection of recyclable materials that technically are not waste, as part of a municipal landfill diversion program.

Household waste in economically developed countries will generally be left in waste containers or recycling bins prior to collection by a waste collector using a waste collection vehicle. However, in many developing countries, such as Mexico and Egypt, waste left in bins or bags at the side of the road will not be removed unless residents interact with the waste collectors. Mexico City residents must haul their trash to a waste collection vehicle which makes frequent stops around each neighborhood. The waste collectors will indicate their readiness by ringing a distinctive bell and possibly shouting. Residents line up and hand their trash container to the waste collector. A tip may be expected in some neighborhoods. Private contractor waste collectors may circulate in the same neighborhoods as many as five times per day, pushing a cart with a waste container, ringing a bell and shouting to announce their presence. These private contractors are not paid a salary and survive only on the tips they receive. Later, they meet up with a waste collection vehicle to deposit their accumulated waste.

The waste collection vehicle will often take the waste to a transfer station where it will be loaded up into a larger vehicle and sent to either a landfill or alternative waste treatment facility.*

-----

26. Which one of the following statements is supported by the preceding passage?

A. In all places in the world, waste is left in bins and is automatically picked up by waste collectors.
   (**NOT CORRECT**. "...in many developing countries, such as Mexico and Egypt, <u>waste left in bins or bags at the side of the road will not be removed unless residents interact with the waste collectors</u>.)

B. The term "waste collection" does not include the pick-up of recyclable materials because "recyclable materials" are not considered waste.
   (**NOT CORRECT**. "Waste collection is a part of the process of waste management...and also <u>includes</u> the curbside collection of recyclable materials that technically are not waste.")

C. In Mexico City trash is picked up at curbside in front of residences.
   (**NOT CORRECT**. "Mexico City residents must <u>haul their trash</u> to a waste collection vehicle which makes frequent stops around each neighborhood.")

D. <u>In Mexico, people sometimes are expected to tip the waste collectors</u>.
   (**CORRECT. THIS IS THE ANSWER.** "Residents line up and hand their trash container to the waste collector. <u>A tip may be expected in some neighborhoods</u>.")

----

27. According to the preceding passage, which of the following statements is <u>not</u> correct?

A. In Mexico, waste collection vehicle will often take the waste to a transfer station.

B. Household waste in economically developed countries will generally be left in waste containers or recycling bins prior to collection by a waste collector using a waste collection vehicle.

C. Waste collection also includes the curbside collection of recyclable materials.

D. <u>In many developing countries, such as Mexico and Egypt, waste left in bins or bags at the side of the road will be removed and the residents do not need to interact with the waste collectors.</u>
   (**NOT CORRECT. THIS IS THE ANSWER.** "...in many developing countries, such as

Mexico and Egypt, waste left in bins or bags at the side of the road <u>will not be removed unless residents interact</u> with the waste collectors.")

28. According to the preceding passage, which of the following statements is correct?

A. Waste collection is the transfer of solid and liquid waste from the point of use and disposal to the point of treatment or landfill.

(**NOT CORRECT**. "Waste collection is a part of the process of waste management. It is the transfer of **<u>solid</u>** waste from the point of use and disposal to the point of treatment or landfill.")

B. Waste collection does not include the curbside collection of recyclable materials that technically are not waste, as part of a municipal landfill diversion program.

(**NOT CORRECT**. "Waste collection also **<u>includes</u>** the curbside collection of recyclable materials that technically are not waste, as part of a municipal landfill diversion program.")

<u>C. In Mexico City, waste collectors will indicate their readiness by ringing a distinctive bell and possibly shouting</u>.

(**CORRECT. THIS IS THE ANSWER.** "Mexico City residents must haul their trash to a waste collection vehicle which makes frequent stops around each neighborhood. The waste collectors will indicate their readiness by <u>ringing a distinctive bell and possibly shouting</u>. Residents line up and hand their trash container to the waste collector.")

D. Household waste in economically underdeveloped countries will generally be left in waste containers or recycling bins prior to collection by a waste collector using a waste collection vehicle.

(**NOT CORRECT**. "Household waste in economically **<u>developed</u>** countries will generally be left in waste containers or recycling bins prior to collection by a waste collector using a waste collection vehicle.")

———————————

Deductive Reasoning Answers 29 - 32

Answer question 29 - 32 based on the information provided in the following "Biohazard Levels" passage.

Biohazard Levels

The United States Centers for Disease Control and Prevention (CDC) categorizes various diseases in levels of biohazard, Level 1 being minimum risk and Level 4 being extreme risk.

Biohazard Level 1:

Bacteria and viruses including Bacillus subtilis, canine hepatitis, Escherichia coli, varicella (chicken pox), as well as some cell cultures and non-infectious bacteria. At this level precautions against the biohazardous materials in question are minimal, most likely involving gloves and some sort of facial protection.

Biohazard Level 2:

Bacteria and viruses that cause only mild disease to humans or are difficult to contract via aerosol in a lab setting, such as hepatitis A, B, and C, influenza A, Lyme disease, salmonella, mumps, measles, scrapie, dengue fever.

Biohazard Level 3:

Bacteria and viruses that can cause severe to fatal disease in humans, but for which vaccines or other treatments exist, such as anthrax, West Nile virus, Venezuelan equine encephalitis, SARS virus, tuberculosis, typhus, Rift Valley fever, HIV, Rocky Mountain spotted fever, yellow fever, and malaria. Among parasites Plasmodium falciparum, which causes Malaria, and Trypanosoma cruzi, which causes trypanosomiasis, also come under this level.

Biohazard Level 4:

Viruses and bacteria that cause severe to fatal disease in humans, and for which vaccines or other treatments are not available, such as Bolivian and Argentine hemorrhagic fevers, Marburg virus, Ebola virus, hantaviruses, Lassa fever virus, Crimean–Congo hemorrhagic fever, and other hemorrhagic diseases. Variola virus (smallpox) is an agent that is worked with at BSL-4 despite the existence of a vaccine. When dealing with biological hazards at this level the use of a positive pressure personnel suit, with a segregated air supply, is mandatory.*

-----

29. According to the preceding "Biohazard Levels" passage, the highest and most dangerous biohazard risk is designated as:

A. Biohazard Level 1

B. Biohazard Level 2

C. Biohazard Level 3

D. Biohazard Level 4

(THIS IS THE CORRECT ANSWER. "The United States Centers for Disease Control and Prevention (CDC) categorizes various diseases in levels of biohazard, Level 1 being minimum risk and Level 4 being extreme risk.")

----

30. A "positive pressure personnel suit" must be used when dealing with Biohazard Level(s):

A. Biohazard Level 1 only

B. Biohazard Levels 1 and 2 only

C. Biohazard Level 1, 2, 3 and 4

D. Biohazard Level 4

(THIS IS THE CORRECT ANSWER. "Biohazard Level 4...When dealing with biological hazards at this level the use of a positive pressure personnel suit, with a segregated air supply, is mandatory.")

----

31. The parasite Plasmodium falciparum, which causes Malaria Malria, comes under Biohazard Level:

A. 1

B. 2

C. 3

(THIS IS THE CORRECT ANSWER. "Biohazard Level 3...Among parasites Plasmodium falciparum, which causes Malaria, and Trypanosoma cruzi, which causes trypanosomiasis, also come under this level.")

D. 4

----

32. Biohazardous materials most likely involving gloves and some sort of facial protection are used most likely when the biohazard level is below level:

A. 2

(THIS IS THE ANSWER. "Biohazard Level 1...At this level precautions against the biohazardous materials in question are minimal, most likely involving gloves and some sort of facial protection.")

B. 3

C. 4

D. 5

Questions 33 Answer

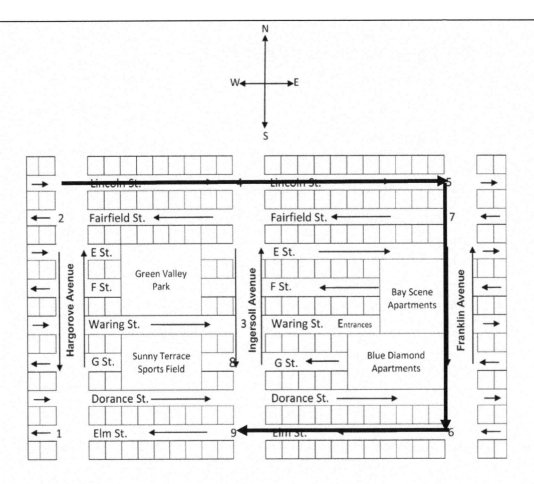

(See dark arrows, above.)

33. Imagine that you are at Hargrove Avenue and Lincoln Street and then drive East to Franklin Avenue, then drive South to Elm St., then travel West to Ingersoll Avenue, you will be closest to which one of the following points?

A. 2   B. 4   C. 5   **D. 9**

Questions 34 Answer

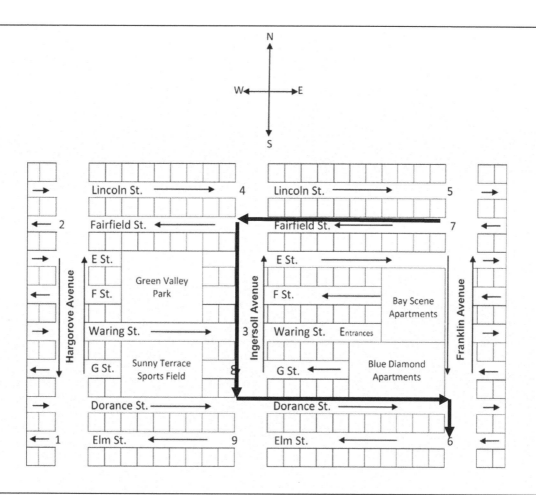

34. If you start your drive at point number 7, then drive West to Ingersoll Avenue, then drive South to Dorance St., then East to Franklin Avenue, then drive South to Elm St., you will be closest to which one of the following point?

A. 1   B. 5   **C. 6**   D. 9

Questions 35 Answer

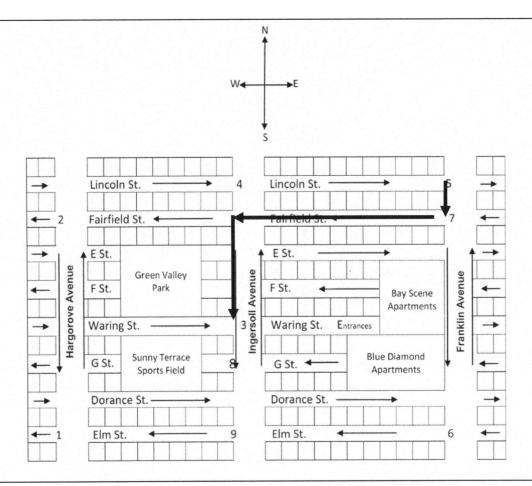

35. You are in your sanitation vehicle at the intersection of Lincoln St. and Franklin Avenue. You are informed that you are needed at the intersection of Waring Street and Ingersoll Avenue. Assuming that you must obey all traffic signs, which one of the following four choices describes the most direct route?

A. Drive South on Franklin Avenue to Fairfield St, then drive East on Fairfield St. to Ingersoll Avenue, then South to the intersection of Waring Street and Ingersoll Avenue.

B. Drive South on Franklin Avenue to Fairfield St, then drive West on Fairfield St. to Ingersoll Avenue, then North to the intersection of Waring Street and Ingersoll Avenue.

C. Drive North on Franklin Avenue to Fairfield St, then drive East on Fairfield St. to Ingersoll Avenue, then North to the intersection of Waring Street and Ingersoll Avenue.

D. Drive South on Franklin Avenue to Fairfield St, then drive West on Fairfield St. to Ingersoll Avenue, then South to the intersection of Waring Street and Ingersoll Avenue.

Questions 36 Answer

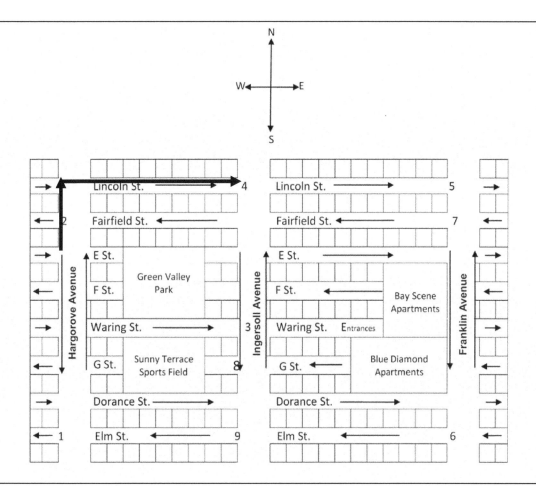

36. You are in your sanitation vehicle at Hargrove Avenue and E St. You are informed that you are needed at the corner of Lincoln St. and Ingersoll Avenue. Which one of the following four choices describes the most direct route?

A. Drive South to Lincoln St. then West on Lincoln St. to the corner of Lincoln St. and Ingersoll Avenue.

B. Drive North to Lincoln St. then East on Lincoln St. to the corner of Lincoln St. and Ingersoll Avenue.

C. Drive South to Dorance St. then East on Dorance St. to Ingersoll Avenue, then North to Lincoln Street. Avenue.

D. Drive North to Lincoln St. then West on Lincoln St. to the corner of Lincoln St. and Ingersoll Avenue.

Spatial Orientation Answers 37 – 42

37. While on waste collection, you and another Sanitation Worker are stopped by an elderly woman who tells you that a "tall man" just threw hazardous medical waste on the sidewalk. You notice a "tall man" calmly walking down the block southbound to the end of the block where he makes a right turn, then observe the man continuing to walk for two blocks before making another right turn.

According to the information in the preceding passage, you would be most correct to inform your supervisor that you last saw the man walking:

A) North

B) South

C) East

D) West

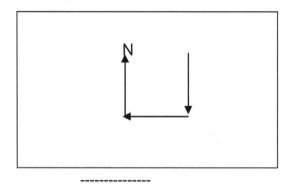

----

38. While in your waste collection vehicle, you notice a car sideswipe a parked car and then drive off northbound without stopping. After four blocks the car makes a right turn and then after two more blocks makes a left turn.

According to the information in the preceding passage, you would be most correct to inform your supervisor that you last saw the car heading:

A) North

B) South

C) East

D) West

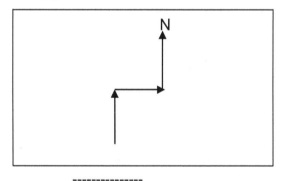

----

39. A jewelry store employee runs out of a jewelry store, points down the block and shouts, "That guy just robbed me!" The man continues running westbound. After three blocks, he make a left turn and runs for two more blocks before making another left turn.

According to the information in the preceding passage, you would be most correct to say that you last saw the suspect heading:

A) North

B) South

C) East

D) West

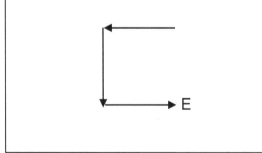

40. You and another witness a private sanitation truck leak noxious liquids on the street. You notice that the private sanitation truck is heading in a westbound direction. You also see that it stays in that direction for three blocks before turning left and then after another block, turns right..

According to the information in the preceding passage, you would be most correct to radio that the private sanitation truck is travelling:

A) North

B) South

C) East

D) West

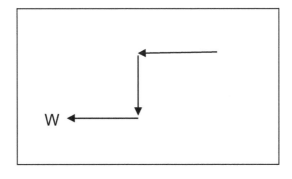

----

41. While in your waste collection vehicle, you witness two men come out of a bar and overturn city owned trash cans, spilling the contents, including broken glass, on the sidewalk. They quickly get into a car and head northbound. After three blocks, they make a right turn and then after two more blocks they make another right turn.

According to the information in the preceding passage, you would be most correct to radio that you last saw the car heading:

A) North

B) South

C) East

D) West

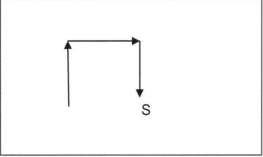

----

42. Your attention is drawn to a pedestrian shouting, "He took my bike!" and pointing to a man on a bike pedaling quickly on the sidewalk, away from the pedestrian and in an westbound direction. After three blocks, he make a right turn and then after two more blocks he makes a left turn.

According to the information in the preceding passage, you would be most correct to tell the police that you last saw the man heading:

A) North

B) South

C) East

D) West

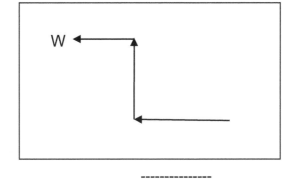

Visualization Answer 43

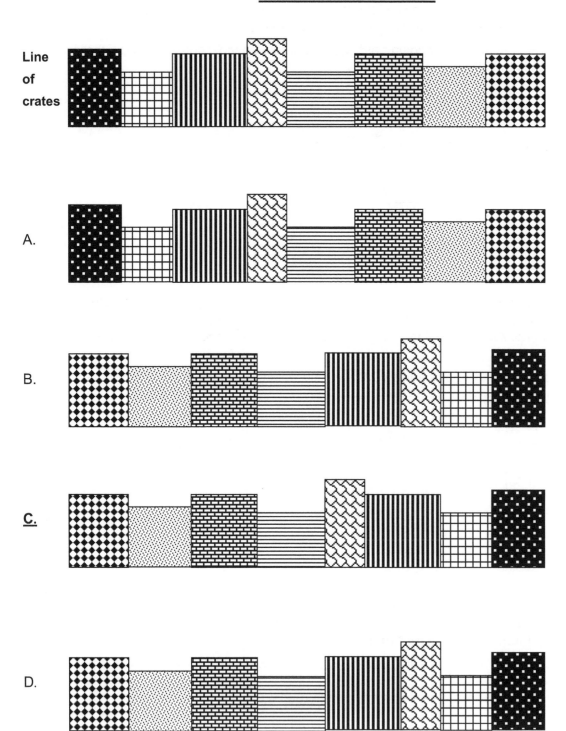

43. The above "Line of Crates" when viewed from the back would appear as which of the following choices?

A. Choice A   **C. Choice C**

B. Choice B   D. Choice D

The answer is "C." (To make the answer clear, we have filled in each corresponding box with the same pattern.)

Visualization Question 44

Which of the following circles (A, B, C, D) matches the image "Dissected Circle?"

A. Image A   C. Image C

B. Image B   D. Image D

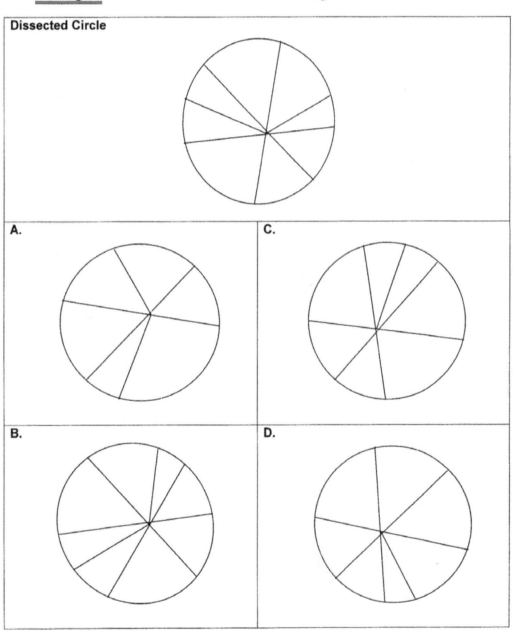

Visualization Answer 45

While driving a NYC Sanitation Department vehicle, Sanitation Worker Abe Jenner is involved in an auto accident. He states that while he was driving on Vine St. in car #3, car #1 hit his rear bumper, causing him to hit vehicle number 2.

Assume that all 3 vehicles were in their proper lanes of traffic.

Which of the following 4 diagrams below best matches the statement of Sanitation Worker Abe Jenner?

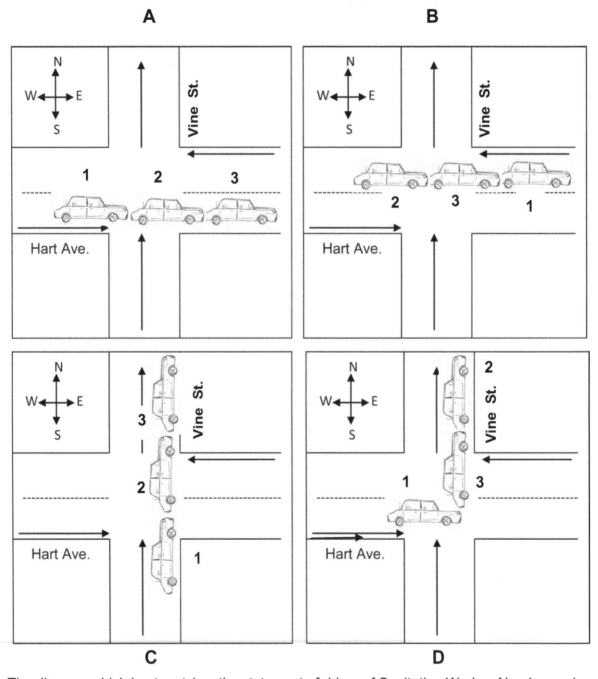

44. The diagram which best matches the statement of driver of Sanitation Worker Abe Jenner is:

A. diagram "A"   C. diagram "C"

B. diagram "B"   **D. diagram "D"**

'The sequence, Car 1 hits car 3 which then hits car 2 is only displayed in Diagram "D.")

Answers 46 - 47

Answer questions 46 – 47 based on the following accident details.

Sanitation Worker Dean Garullo collects the following information at the scene of an auto accident in which he was involved while driving a 2008 Toyota Sienna owned by the NYC Dept. of Sanitation.

Date of Accident: September 9, 2019
Time of accident: 4:15 p.m.
Place of accident: Intersection of Lavin Avenue and Reiker Avenue, Bronx
Driver: Sanitation Worker Dean Garullo. Owner: NYC Dept. of Sanitation
Vehicle: 2008 Toyota Sienna
Damage: Vehicle struck a commercial metal garbage container protruding into the street, causing damage to the front bumper.

-----

46. Sanitation Worker Dean Garullo is preparing a report of the accident and has four drafts of the report. He wishes to use the draft that expresses the information most clearly, accurately and completely. Which draft should he choose?

A. At 4:15 p.m., on September 9, 2019, at the intersection of Lavin Avenue and Riker Avenue, Bronx, a vehicle driven by Sanitation Worker Dean Garullo and owned by the NYC Dept. of Sanitation, struck a commercial metal garbage container protruding into the street, causing damage to the front bumper. **(Type of vehicle is not stated)**

B. On **September 7, 2019**, at 4:15 p.m., at the intersection of Lavin Avenue and Reiker Avenue, Bronx, a 2008 Toyota Sienna driven by Sanitation Worker Dean Garullo and owned by the NYC Dept. of Sanitation, struck a commercial metal garbage container protruding into the street, causing damage to the front bumper. **(Date is wrong.)**

C. On September 9, 2019, at **4:25 p.m.**, at the intersection of Lavin Avenue and Reiker Avenue, Bronx, a 2008 Toyota Sienna driven by Sanitation Worker Dean Garullo and owned by the NYC Dept. of Sanitation, struck a commercial metal garbage container protruding into the street, causing damage to the front bumper. **(Time is wrong)**

D. On September 9, 2019, at 4:15 p.m., at the intersection of Lavin Avenue and Reiker Avenue, Bronx, a 2008 Toyota Sienna driven by Sanitation Worker Dean Garullo and

owned by the NYC Dept. of Sanitation, struck a commercial metal garbage container protruding into the street, causing damage to the front bumper. (Correct Summary)

----

47. Sanitation Worker Dean Garullo is comparing the information he recorded in his memo pad (at the scene of the accident) to the information in his report. Which of the above choices (A, B, C or D) has one detail that does <u>not</u> agree with the information in the Sanitation Worker's memo pad?

A. Date of Accident: September 9, 2019; Time of accident: 4:15 p.m.

B. Place of accident: Intersection of Lavin Avenue and Reiker Avenue, Bronx

C. Driver: Dean Garullo: Vehicle: 2008 Toyota Sienna

D. Damage: Vehicle struck a commercial plastic garbage container protruding into the street. (Correct Summary. Container was metal, not plastic.**)**

Answer questions 48 and 49 based on the following information gathered at a crime scene.

Sanitation Worker Henrietta Ferguson discovers that her official NYC Sanitation Department vehicle has been stolen. She gathers the following information:

Suspect: Unidentified

Date of crime: August 25, 2019

Time of crime: between 7:20 p.m. and 11:40 p.m.

Crime: theft of car

Vehicle stolen: 2012 Volvo

Owner: NYC Department of Sanitation

Driver: Sanitation Worker Henrietta Ferguson

Place of crime: driveway in front of 247 18th Street, Staten Island

-----

48. Sanitation Worker Henrietta Ferguson is preparing a report of the accident and has prepared four drafts of the report. She wishes to use the draft that expresses the information most clearly, accurately and completely. Which of the following drafts should she choose?

A. A car theft of a 2012 Volvo happened at the driveway in front of 247 18th Street, Staten Island, Staten Island where the NYC Department of Sanitation vehicle was parked. The alleged thief is unidentified, as the theft happened in the evening hours. **(date is missing, time is missing, sloppy language)**

B. On August 25, 2019, between 7:20 p.m. and 11:40 p.m., at the driveway in front of 247 18th Street, Staten Island, a 2012 Volvo owned by the NYC Department of Sanitation and driven by Sanitation Worker Henrietta Ferguson, was stolen by an unidentified suspect. (CORRECT)

C. A car was stolen on August 25, 2019, between 7:20 p.m. and 11:40 p.m., at the driveway in front of 247 18th Street, Staten Island, owned by Dept. of Sanitation. The suspect is unidentified. **(no type of car, sloppy language)**

D. On August 25, 2019, 247 18th Street, Staten Island, between 7:20 **a.m.** and 11:40 **a.m.**, a 2012 Volvo owned by the NYC Dept. of Sanitation was stolen by an unidentified suspect. **(wrong time, driver name missing)**

----

49. Sanitation Worker Henrietta Ferguson is comparing the information she recorded in her memo pad (at the scene of the crime) to the information in her report. Which of the above choices (A, B, C or D) has one detail that does <u>not</u> agree with the information in the Sanitation Worker's memo pad?

A. Date of crime: August 25, 2019; Time of crime: between 7:20 p.m. and 11:40 p.m.

B. Crime: theft of car; Vehicle stolen: 2012 Volvo

C. Victim: owner of car: NYC Department of Sanitation; Driver: Sanitation Worker Henrietta Ferguson

D. Place of crime: driveway in front of 247 18th Avenue, Staten Island (should be "Street.")

Answer question 50 - 51 based on the following "Media Inquiry Procedure."

Media Inquiry Procedure

When a criminal case is pending in the courts, a Sanitation Worker who may be called to be a witness is prohibited from discussing the case with any newspaper, magazine, TV reporters and all other media. Exceptions to this are cases where:

1. a New York court of competent jurisdiction formally orders the Sanitation Worker to discuss one or more particulars of the case.

2. a NYPD authorized Department orders such discussion

3. the Sanitation Worker is subpoenaed to testify by an authorized NYC, NYS or federal board. Media inquiries made to the Sanitation Officer should be referred to HQ Media Services at One Police Plaza.

-----

50. Sanitation Worker June Halister discovers 80 pounds of heroin in a garbage dumpster. A suspect is found, indicted, and now is in jail, waiting for trial. A newspaper reporter, Abigail Briggs, contacts Sanitation Worker June Halister and asks a quick question, the answer to which might help the reporter to investigate drug trafficking in the city. Sanitation Worker June Halister should:

A. answer the question since it is a quick question.

B. tell the reporter to contact her supervisor.

C. answer the question only if the reporter is trustworthy.

D. tell the reporter to contact HQ Media Services at One Police Plaza.

----

51. Sanitation Worker June Halister is subpoenaed to testify by an authorized federal board regarding the 80 pounds of heroin that she discovered. Based on the above, "Media Inquiry Procedure," Sanitation Worker June Halister should:

A. disregard the subpoena as it is from a federal board and she is a NYC employee.

B. call the reporter an inform her of the subpoena.

C. call in sick on the day of the subpoena in order to not testify, as per "Media Inquiry Procedure."

D. Inform her supervisor and obey the subpoena.

Information Ordering Questions 52 - 54

If a waste collection truck breaks down, the Sanitation Worker assigned to drive the truck should first notify the local headquarters. The driver should relay the truck ID number, the location of the truck, and the suspected problem with the truck. Neither the driver nor his partner on the assignment should attempt to fix the truck. Both the driver and his partner should remain with the truck and be present when the repair detail comes to repair the truck. As soon as the truck is repaired, the driver should notify the local headquarters. He should also notify the local headquarters when garbage pickup resumes. The driver, either at the scene or upon the return to the garage, must enter all the pertinent information in the truck's daily journal.

52. Based on the preceding procedures, after relaying to headquarters the truck ID number, the location of the truck, and the suspected problem with the truck described above, the next thing the driver or his partner should do is:

A. relay to headquarters the names of the repair crew.

B. attempt to fix the truck

C. notify local headquarters of the vehicle break-down.

D. remain with the truck.

53. The sanitation worker working with the driver must enter all the pertinent information in the truck's daily journal:

A. only at the scene

B. only upon return to the garage

C. at the scene or upon the return to the garage

D. none of the above

54. After the truck is repaired, what is the next step that should be taken?

A. resume the garbage collection route.

B. take the truck on at least a ten minute drive to evaluate its performance.

C. the driver should notify the local headquarters.

D. none of the above

———————

Information Ordering Questions 55 - 57

The following five sentences (listed in random order) are the five necessary steps to properly record and process a Sanitation Worker's pre-approved overtime. Which one of the following choices (A, B, C, D) lists the order of sentences which best expresses the logical sequence of the proper recording and processing of pre-approved overtime?

1. A the end of the bi-weekly pay period, record the Overtime Worked Report Confirmation Number in section 2 of the Bi-Weekly Pay Period Report.

2. Sign the Bi-Weekly Pay Period Report and submit it to the Local Sanitation Station.

3. After the approved overtime work shift, submit to the local Sanitation Station a completed "Overtime Worked Report" and obtain an Overtime Worked Report Confirmation Number for its submission.

4. Obtain pre-approval from the local Sanitation Station.

5. Work the number of overtime hours requested on the approved overtime pre-approval form.

55. Which of the following choices lists the most logical sequence of steps for the proper recording and processing of pre-approved overtime?

A. 5, 1 ,3 ,2, 4

B. 4, 5, 3, 1, 2

C. 5, 1, 4, 3, 2

D. 5, 4, 1, 3, 2

Question 55 Answer: B. 4, 5, 3, 1, 2

4. Obtain pre-approval from the local Sanitation Station.

5. Work the number of overtime hours requested on the approved overtime pre-approval form.

3. After the approved overtime work shift, submit to the local Sanitation Station a completed "Overtime Worked Report" and obtain an Overtime Worked Report Confirmation Number for its submission.

1. A the end of the bi-weekly pay period, record the Overtime Worked Report Confirmation Number in section 2 of the Bi-Weekly Pay Period Report.

2. Sign the Bi-Weekly Pay Period Report and submit it to the Local Sanitation Station.

56. According to the above steps for the proper recording and processing of pre-approved overtime, the periodic Pay Period Report must be submitted to the Local Sanitation Station:

A. every day

B. every week

C. every month

D. none of the above (Must be submitted bi-weekly.)

57. According to the above steps for the recording and processing of pre-approved overtime, which of the following statements is not correct?

A. Pre-approval for the overtime is obtained from the local Sanitation Station.

B. The Bi-Weekly Pay Period Report is signed by the Sanitation Worker.

C. The pay-period is bi-weekly.

D. An Overtime Worked Report Confirmation Number must be obtained prior to working overtime. (This is not correct because the number is obtained after working overtime.)

Information Ordering Questions 58 - 60

The following are four sentences. Each sentence (listed in random order) is one of the four steps necessary to sign-out a snow plow at the Sanitation Department garage at the beginning of a shift.

1. Locate the assigned snow plow and visually inspect it for any obvious defects or missing equipment.

2. Drive slowly out of the garage to make sure that the Snow Plow is in good operational order and does not have mechanical defects..

3. Sign the "Snow Plow Assignment Log" at the Superintendent's office and obtain the keys to the Snow Plow."

4. Obtain from the garage superintendent the ID number of the snow plow assigned to you.

58. Which one of the following choices (A, B, C, D) lists the order of sentences which best expresses the logical sequence of signing-out for a snow plow?

A. 1, 4, 2, 3   **C. 4, 1, 3, 2**

B. 2, 3, 4, 1   D. 3, 4, 2, 1

4. Obtain from the garage superintendent the ID number of the snow plow assigned to you.

1. Locate the assigned snow plow and visually inspect it for any obvious defects or missing equipment.

3. Sign the "Snow Plow Assignment Log" at the Superintendent's office and obtain the keys to the Snow Plow."

2. Drive slowly out of the garage to make sure that the Snow Plow is in good operational order and does not have mechanical defects.

59. According to the above Snow Plow Sign-Out procedure, the snow plow should be inspected for mechanical defects:

A. in the morning.

B. in the afternoon.

C. in the evening.

D. none of the above (The snow plow should be checked for mechanical defects when driving slowly out of the garage.)

60 According to the above procedure, which of the following is <u>not</u> correct?

A. The License plate number of the snow plow assigned to you is obtained from the garage superintendent. (The **ID number** of the snow plow is obtained from the garage superintendent.)

B. The "Snow Plow Assignment Log" is signed by the driver.

C. Drive slowly out of the garage to make sure that the Snow Plow is in good operational order and does not have mechanical defects.

D. Locate the assigned snow plow and visually inspect it for any obvious defects or missing equipment.

END

SANITATION WORKER EXAM 2020 – NEW YORK CITY

Answer Key - Test 1

1. C	21. B	41. B
2. B	22. B	42. D
3. C	23. C	43. C
4. C	24. A	44. B
5. D	25. D	45. D
6. C	26. D	46. D
7. C	27. D	47. D
8. C	28. C	48. B
9. B	29. D	49. D
10. D	30. D	50. D
11. B	31. C	51. D
12. C	32. A	52. D
13. D	33. D	53. C
14. A	34. C	54. C
15. D	35. D	55. B
16. D	36. B	56. D
17. D	37. A	57. D
18. C	38. A	58. C
19. D	39. C	59. D
20. C	40. D	60. A

PRACTICE TEST #2 QUESTIONS

Reading Comprehension

Question 1:

The New York City Department of Sanitation, or DSNY, is the city agency responsible for garbage collection, recycling collection, street cleaning, and snow removal. It employs a uniformed force of unionized sanitation workers (Local 831 USA of the Teamsters) in New York City. Like the rest of New York's uniformed forces, they have a nickname: "New York's Strongest." The section of Worth Street between Centre and Baxter Streets in Manhattan is named "Avenue of the Strongest" in their honor.

The New York City Department of Sanitation is the largest sanitation department in the world, with 7,200 uniformed sanitation workers and supervisors, 2,041 civilian workers, 2,230 collection trucks, 275 specialized collection trucks, 450 street sweepers, 365 salt and sand spreaders, 298 front end loaders, 2,360 support vehicles, and handles over 12,000 tons of residential and institutional refuse and recyclables a day.*

1. Which of the following statements is best supported by the preceding paragraph?
A. All New York City Department of Sanitation (DSNY) employees are members of Local 831 of the Teamsters.
B. The DSNY has 365 salt and sand spreaders and 465 specialized collection trucks.
C. The DSNY does not employ civilian workers.
D. Snow removal is a responsibility of the DSNY.

Question 2:

The DSNY was founded in 1881 as the Department of Street Cleaning. One of the Department's first Commissioners, Colonel George E. Waring, Jr., pioneered such current practices as recycling, street sweeping, and a dedicated uniformed cleaning and collection force.

The New York City Department of Sanitation has its own police force, which is composed of four specialized units: The Uniformed Sanitation Police Force, The Illegal Dumping Task Force, The Permit and Inspection Unit, and The Environmental Police Unit. They are composed of uniformed and undercover officers who handle sanitation related emergency calls, and enforce sanitation related laws in addition to state and city traffic and criminal laws in the 5 boroughs of New York City.

The DSNY police officers are NYS peace officer certified by the NYS Municipal Training Council. Officers may carry a firearm, carry and use handcuffs, make warrantless arrests, issue summonses, and use physical and deadly force. The police force uses marked and unmarked police cars.*

2. According to the preceding passage, which of the following statements is correct?
A. DSNY police officers are not authorized to carry firearms.
B. Colonel George C. Harding pioneered such current practices as recycling, street sweeping, and a dedicated uniformed cleaning and collection force.
C. A DSNY police officer can arrest someone without having in his possession a warrant of arrest.
D. The DSNY police force is composed of uniformed officers only.

Questions 3:
Throughout most of history, the amount of waste generated by humans was insignificant due to low population density and low societal levels of the exploitation of natural resources. Common waste produced during pre-modern times was mainly ashes and human biodegradable waste, and these were released back into the ground locally, with minimum environmental impact. Tools made out of wood or metal were generally reused or passed down through the generations.

However, some civilizations do seem to have been more profligate in their waste output than others. In particular, the Maya of Central America had a fixed monthly ritual in which the people of the village would gather together and burn their rubbish in large dumps.*

3. According to the above selection, which of the following statements is correct?:
A. Throughout all of history, all waste has been mainly ashes and human biodegradable waste.
B. Tools made out of wood or metal were generally discarded after use.

C. Ashes released back into the ground locally had a major environmental impact.

D. The Maya of Central America burned their rubbish in large dumps.

Question 4:

Wagons and other means had been used for centuries to haul away solid waste. Trucks were first used for this purpose soon after their invention. The 1920s saw the first open-topped trucks being used, but due to foul odors and waste falling from the back, covered vehicles soon became more common. These covered trucks were first introduced in more densely populated Europe and then in North America, but were soon used worldwide.

The main difficulty was that the waste collectors needed to lift the waste to shoulder height. The first technique developed in the late 20s to solve this problem was to build round compartments with massive corkscrews that would lift the load and bring it away from the rear. A more efficient model was the development of the hopper in 1929. It used a cable system that could pull waste into the truck.*

4. Which of the following titles expresses the main idea of the above passage?

A. The History of Sanitation Workers

B. The History of Waste Collection Vehicles

C. The Future of Waste Collection Vehicles

D. Waste Collection Vehicles of South America

Question 5:

Waste can be classified in several ways but the following list represents a typical classification:

Biodegradable waste: food and kitchen waste, green waste, paper (can also be recycled)

Recyclable material: paper, glass, bottles, cans, metals, certain plastics, fabrics, clothes, batteries etc.

Inert waste: construction and demolition waste, dirt, rocks, debris

Electrical and electronic waste (WEEE): electrical appliances, TVs, computers, screens, etc.

Composite wastes: waste clothing, Tetra Packs, waste plastics such as toys

Hazardous waste: including most paints, chemicals, light bulbs, fluorescent tubes, spray cans, fertilizer and containers

Toxic waste: including pesticide, herbicides, fungicides

Medical waste.*

5. Which of the following classification of the item stated is not supported by the above waste classification?

A. light bulbs: "Hazardous waste including most paints"

B. pesticide: "Toxic waste"

C. paper: "Biodegradable waste"

D. glass: "Inert waste"

Question 6:

Municipal solid waste can be used to generate energy. Several technologies have been developed that make the processing of MSW for energy generation cleaner and more economical than ever before, including landfill gas capture, combustion, pyrolysis, gasification, and plasma arc gasification. While older waste incineration plants emitted high levels of pollutants, recent regulatory changes and new technologies have significantly reduced this concern. United States Environmental Protection Agency (EPA) regulations in 1995 and 2000 under the Clean Air Act have succeeded in reducing emissions of dioxins from waste-to-energy facilities by more than 99 percent below 1990 levels, while mercury emissions have been by over 90 percent. The EPA noted these improvements in 2003, citing waste-to-energy as a power source "with less environmental impact than almost any other source of electricity."*

6. Based on the subject matter of the preceding passage, the most appropriate meaning for "MSW" is:

A. Manually Selected Waste

B. Municipal Solid Waste

C. Marked Selected Waste

D. Manifest Solid Waste

Question 7:

Waste segregation means dividing waste into dry and wet. Dry waste includes wood and related products, metals and glass. Wet waste, typically refers to organic waste usually generated by eating establishments and are heavy in weight due to dampness. Waste can also be segregated on basis of biodegradable or non-biodegradable waste.*

7. According to the above passage, which of the following statements is correct?

A. An empty aluminum cola can is considered wet waste.

B. A half-eaten apple is considered non-biodegradable waste.

C. Wood is considered wet waste.

D. A wooden broom handle is considered dry waste.

Question 8:

Incineration is a waste treatment process that involves the combustion of organic substances contained in waste materials. Incineration and other high-temperature waste treatment systems are described as "thermal treatment". Incineration of waste materials converts the waste into ash, flue gas, and heat. The ash is mostly formed by the inorganic constituents of the waste, and may take the form of solid lumps or particulates carried by the flue gas. The flue gases must be cleaned of gaseous and particulate pollutants before they are dispersed into the atmosphere. In some cases, the heat generated by incineration can be used to generate electric power.*

8. According to the preceding passage, which of the following statements is correct?
A. Incineration involves the combustion of inorganic substances.
B. Incineration of waste materials converts the waste into atomic energy.
C. Ash is mostly formed by the organic constituents of waste.
D. In some cases, electric power can be generated from the heat generated by incineration.

_____

Written Expression Questions 9 - 18

9. A Sanitation Worker is reviewing a report she is preparing. It contains the following two rough drafts. Which of the two sentences are grammatically correct?

1. Man who commended Sanitation Worker Gail Robertson about thirty years old was wearing a business suit.

2. The man who commended Sanitation Worker Gail Robertson was about thirty years old and was wearing a business suit.

A. Only sentence 1 is grammatically correct.

B. Only sentence 2 is grammatically correct.

C. Both sentence 1 and 2 are grammatically correct.

D. Neither sentence 1 nor sentence 2 is grammatically correct.

----

10. A Sanitation Worker is asked by his partner to review a speech that the Sanitation Worker has volunteered to give to a fifth grade class. It contains the following two versions of one part of the speech. Which versions are grammatically correct?

1. Recycling is important it helps the environment it creates job opportunities.

2. Recycling is important because it helps the environment and creates job opportunities.

A. Only sentence 1 is grammatically correct.

B. Only sentence 2 is grammatically correct.

C. Both sentence 1 and 2 are grammatically correct.

D. Neither sentence 1 nor sentence 2 is grammatically correct.

----

11. A Sanitation Worker is preparing a report and has not decided which of two versions of a specific section he wishes to use. Which of the two versions are grammatically correct?

1. The alleged violator and his alleged accomplice have decided not to speak with the Enviromental Control Officer. Both stated that they will not cooperate in any manner.
spelled wrong

2. Both the aleged violator and his alleged accomplice stated that they will not cooperate in any way and that they will not speak with the Environmental Control Officer.

A. Only sentence 1 is grammatically correct.

B. Only sentence 2 is grammatically correct.

C. Both sentence 1 and 2 are grammatically correct.

D) Neither sentence 1 nor sentence 2 is grammatically correct.

12. Sanitation Worker Dino Foster is preparing a speech that he will give at a recruiting session which his supervisor has asked him to attend. Which of the following two version are grammatically correct?

> 1. Sanitation Workers exert themselves physically every day they need to eat healthy foods and maintain a healthy life style.

> 2. Sanitation Workers exert themselves physically every day. They need to eat healthy foods and maintain a healthy life style

A. 1 only is correct.

B. 2 only is correct.

C) Neither 1 nor 2 is correct.

D. Both 1 and 2 are correct.

----

13. Sanitation Worker Brenda Rodriguez is preparing an instruction sheet on how to deal with difficult people. Which of the following two sentences are correct?

> 1. When dealing with difficult people, a Sanitation Worker should keep in mind that patience and tact are both very important.

> 2. When a Sanitation Worker deals with difficult people, she should keep in mind that patience and tact are both very important.

A. 1 only is correct.

B. 2 only is correct.

C. Neither 1 nor 2 is correct.

D. Both 1 and 2 are correct.

----

14. Sanitation Worker Felix Ming is checking the correctness of sentences in one of his reports. Which of the following two versions are correct?

1. Because Sanitation Workers are uniformed personel, they are required to maintain their uniforms in a clean and acceptable condition.

2. Sanitation Workers are uniformed personnel they are required to maintain their uniforms in a clean and acceptable condition.

A. 1 only is correct.
B. 2 only is correct.
C. Neither 1 nor 2 is correct.
D. Both 1 and 2 are correct.

----

15. Sanitation Worker Beverly Ming needs to select the best summary (A, B, C or D) of the following information: (The best summary is the one that expresses the information in the most clear, accurate and complete manner.)

Place of accident: in front of 3645 South 82nd Avenue, Brooklyn

Time of accident: 9:45 P.M.

Date of accident: November 15, 2019

Vehicle involved: 2006 Ford Fusion

Driver: Sanitation Worker Beverly Ming

Owner: NYC Dept. of Sanitation

Damage: cracked front bumper

Details: a private metal garbage dumpster rolled into the street and struck the 2006 Ford Fusion

-----

A. On November 15, 2019, 2019, at 9:45 A.M., in front of 3645 South 82nd Avenue, Brooklyn, a metal private garbage dumpster rolled into the street and struck the 2006 Ford Fusion owned by the NYC Dept. of Sanitation and driven by Beverly Ming, resulting in a cracked front bumper.

B. On November 15, 2019, 2019, at 9:45 P.M., in front of 3645 South 82nd Avenue, Brooklyn, a metal private garbage dumpster rolled into the street and struck the 2009 Ford Fusion owned by the NYC Dept. of Sanitation and driven by Sanitation Worker Beverly Ming, resulting in a cracked front bumper.

C. On November 15, 2019, 2019, at 9:45 P.M., in front of 3645 South 82nd Avenue, Brooklyn, a metal private garbage dumpster rolled into the street and struck the 2006 Ford Fusion, driven by Sanitation Worker Beverly Ming, resulting in a cracked front bumper.

D. On November 15, 2019, at 9:45 P.M., in front of 3645 South 82nd Avenue, Brooklyn, a metal private garbage dumpster rolled into the street and struck the 2006 Ford Fusion owned by the NYC Dept. of Sanitation and driven by Sanitation Worker Beverly Ming, resulting in a cracked front bumper.

----

16. Sanitation Worker George Vasilios obtains the following information at the scene of a traffic accident:

Date of accident: November 10, 2019
Time of accident: 6:15 P.M.
Place of accident: intersection of 9th Avenue and 64th Street, New York
Vehicles involved: 2008 Chevrolet Malibu and 2006 Nissan Altima (owned by NYC Dept of Sanitation)
Drivers: Harry Belmont (2008 Chevrolet Malibu) and George Vasilios (2006 Nissan Altima)
Damage: dent on front passenger door of 2006 Nissan Altima

Sanitation Worker George Vasilios drafts four versions to express the above information. Which of the following four versions is most clear, accurate and complete?

A. On November 10, 2019, at 6:15 P.M., at the intersection of 9th Avenue and 64th Street, New York, a 2008 Chevrolet Malibu and a 2006 Nissan Altima were involved in a traffic accident. The 2006 Nissan Altima, owned by the NYC Dept. of Sanitation and driven by Sanitation Worker George Vasilios, sustained a dent on the passenger's front door. The 2008 Chevrolet Malibu, owned by Harry Belmont, did not sustain any damage.

B. On November 10, 2019, at 6:15 A.M., at the intersection of 9th Avenue and 64th Street, New York, a 2008 Chevrolet Malibu and a 2006 Nissan Altima were involved in a traffic accident. The 2006 Nissan Altima, owned by the NYC Dept. of Sanitation and driven by Sanitation

Worker George Vasilios, sustained a dent on the passenger's front door. The 2008 Chevrolet Malibu, driven by Harry Belmont, did not sustain any damage.

C. On November 10, 2019, at 6:15 P.M., at the intersection of 9th Avenue and 64th Street, New York, a 2008 Chevrolet Malibu and a 2006 Nissan Altima were involved in a traffic accident. The 2006 Nissan Altima, owned by the NYC Dept. of Sanitation and driven by Sanitation Worker George Vasilios, sustained a dent on the passenger's front door. The 2008 Chevrolet Malibu, driven by Harry Belmont, did not sustain any damage.

D. On November 10, 2019, at 6:15 P.M., at the intersection of 9th Avenue and 64th Street, New York, a 2006 Chevrolet Malibu and a 2008 Nissan Altima were involved in a traffic accident. The 2008 Nissan Altima, owned by the NYC Dept. of Sanitation and driven by Sanitation Worker George Vasilios, sustained a dent on the passenger's front door. The 2006 Chevrolet Malibu, driven by Harry Belmont, did not sustain any damage.

----

17. Which of the following words is spelled correctly?
A. acceptible
B. colum
C. licence
D. occurrence

----

18. Which of the following four sentences does not have a grammatical error?
A. The personnel department is mailing out the form they want everyone to get it as soon as possible.
B. The Sanitation Supervisor and the Community District Leader has the same goal in mind.
C. Although he wanted to eat a sugar donut, he decided not to order it.
D. He went to the beach and enjoyed himself their.

Problem Sensitivity Questions 19 - 25

19. A person (male, white, about five feet nine inches tall and wearing a black T-shirt, dark pants, and an "Atlantic City'" baseball cap) has been seen spraying the initials "SDP" on the sides of waste collection trucks. Your Sanitation Supervisor asks you to be vigilant for a person fitting that description.

According to the information provided by your supervisor, you should: (Choose the best answer.)

A. report to your supervisor all males and females on your route.

B. report to your supervisor all males and females wearing dark pants.

C. report to your supervisor all persons with the height of five feet nine inches.

D. report to your supervisor all males on the street who are wearing an "Atlantic City" baseball cap and are about five feet nine inches tall and are wearing a black T-shirt.

----

20. Sanitation Worker Karen Cohen notices that a fire hydrant has been opened and water is gushing out of it. Sanitation Worker Karen Cohen should:

A. immediately run into a nearby store and see if they have any information regarding the fire hydrant.

B. take a plastic bag and throw it over the hydrant, as this will limit the amount of gushing water.

C. warn everyone to stay clear and contact the proper authorities.

D. observe the fire hydrant for at least fifteen minutes to see if the flow of water stops by itself before doing anything.

----

21. During his daily refuse collection shift, Sanitation Worker David Callahan discovers that smoke is coming out of the side of his truck. It has the odor of burning electrical wires. Based on the preceding information, what is the first step that Sanitation Worker David Callahan should take?

A. Stop by his friend's local gas station and ask him to take a look at the problem.

B. Stop the truck in a safe spot and warn all persons and traffic to keep away from the truck and immediately notify his supervisor.

C. Keep driving as there is a possibility that the problem may resolve itself.

D. Call the manufacturer of the truck and complain.

----

22. Your supervisor asks you to speak with a Mr. John Forester, residing at 1582 Oak Street (Private House), regarding a complaint that his next door neighbor, residing at 1582 Oak Street (Private House), is continually throwing his garbage on top of Mr. Forester's garbage cans. You immediately notice that your supervisor is providing the same address for both neighbors. What is the first step you should take in this situation?

A. Go to 1582 Oak Street and speak with Mr. Forester regarding his complaint.

B. Ask your supervisor for clarification of the addresses.

C. Disregard your supervisor's instructions because they are obviously confused.

D. Do not ask questions of your supervisor, as he might get upset.

----

23. Sanitation Worker Donna Harmon is on duty when a shop owner runs out of his store and says that one of his customers has just collapsed and is unconscious on the floor.

Based on the preceding information, what should Sanitation Worker Harmon do first?

A. Tell the man to return to the store and not create panic in the streets.

B. Interview all nearby persons to determine if any of them are related to the unconscious person in the store.

C. Apply first aid and CPR if needed and call for medical assistance and police.

D. Sanitation Worker Harmon should not do anything as she is working on waste collection.

----

24. Prior to the start of your waste collection tour, your supervisor gives the name and address of an elderly female who complained that her sidewalk has litter that is produced when the Sanitation Workers empty the contents of her waste containers into their waste collection vehicle. He asks that you speak with her so that she can provide more information. From past experiences, you know that this female is prone to making constant unfounded complaints. What is the first step you should take?

A. Carry out the instructions of your supervisor.

B. Don't speak with the female, as this would be a waste of time.

C. Prepare a report that includes that the woman is prone to making constant complaints and that because of that there was no need to speak with her.

D. Check with her neighbors to see if she has any mental illness.

----

25. Your supervisor informs you that you and your partner will have to use Truck #26 for your waste pickup shift. It is the same truck that you turned in the day before because you and your partner caught a bug (on a piece of clear plastic adhesive tape) and turned it in to your supervisor for examination because you thought it was a bed bug. Today your supervisor informs you that the bug has been examined by the DSNY and found to be a common beetle and not a bed bug. As you are driving off, your partner discovers another similar bug and with a piece of clear plastic adhesive tape captures it.

Based on the preceding, what is the best course for you to follow?

A. Turn in the bug to your supervisor and then follow any direction he may gave you.

B. Stop the truck and go home, as the situation is unhealthy.

C. Take the bug to your friend who is an exterminator and ask for his opinion.

D. Inform your supervisor that both you and your partner will not work today because of the bug infestation.

Deductive Reasoning Questions 26 - 27

Answer question 26 - 27 based on the information provided in the following "Pesticides Regulations."

Pesticides Regulations

Pesticides intended for import into the U.S. require a complete Notice of Arrival (NOA) through U.S. Customs and Border Protection. If this NOA is not complete the product would not make it through customs. The NOA lists the identity of the product, the amount within the package, the date of arrival, and where it can be inspected. There are also other rules listed below:

It must comply with standards set with the U.S. pesticide law.

The pesticide has to be registered with the EPA, except if it's on the exemption list.

It cannot be adulterated or violative.

There must be proper labelling.

The product must have been produced in an EPA registered establishment that files annually.

Pesticides intended for export to other parts of the world do not have a registration requirement under certain conditions. The conditions are as follows:

The foreign purchaser has to submit a statement to the EPA stating it knows the product is not registered and can't be sold on U.S. soil.

The pesticide must contain a label that includes "Not Registered for Use in the United States."

The label requirements must be met, and the label must contain the English language and the language of the receiving country(ies).

The pesticide must comply with all FIFRA establishment registration and reporting requirements.

It must comply with FIFRA record-keeping requirements.*

-----

26. Your supervisor hands you an aerosol can to use as a pesticide in your waste collection truck in the event that you notice any rats. The can does not have a label, but your supervisor assures you it has been imported from a reputable Swiss company.

According to the preceding passage, which of the following statements is correct?

A. The can does not need a label because it is imported from a reputable Swiss company.

B. If the product did have a label, it must also have been registered with the Swiss Export Department.

C. A pesticide that is manufactured for export to Switzerland must contain a label that includes the wording "Not Registered for Use in the United States."

D. Pesticides intended for import into the U.S. do not have to comply with the standards set with the U.S. pesticide law.

----

27. According to the preceding passage, which of the following statements is correct?

A. Pesticides imported into the US must have proper labelling, with the following words included: "Not Registered for Use in the United States."

B. Pesticides imported into the US must comply with the Geneva Pesticides Minimum Standards Act.

C. Pesticides intended for import into the U.S. must have been produced in an EPA registered establishment that files annually.

D. Pesticides intended for import into the U.S. do not require a complete Notice of Arrival (NOA).

Deductive Reasoning Questions 28 - 32

Answer question 28 - 32 based on the information provided in the following "Protective Clothing" passage.

Protective Clothing

Personal protective equipment (PPE) refers to protective clothing, helmets, goggles, or other garments or equipment designed to protect the wearer's body from injury. The hazards addressed by protective equipment include physical, electrical, heat, chemicals, biohazards, and airborne particulate matter. Protective equipment may be worn for job-related occupational safety and health purposes, as well as for sports and other recreational activities. "Protective clothing" is applied to traditional categories of clothing, and "protective gear" applies to items such as pads, guards, shields, or masks, and others.

The purpose of personal protective equipment is to reduce employee exposure to hazards when engineering and administrative controls are not feasible or effective to reduce these risks to acceptable levels. PPE is needed when there are hazards present. PPE has the serious limitation that it does not eliminate the hazard at source and may result in employees being exposed to the hazard if the equipment fails.

Any item of PPE imposes a barrier between the wearer/user and the working environment. This can create additional strains on the wearer; impair their ability to carry out their work and create significant levels of discomfort. Any of these can discourage wearers from using PPE correctly, therefore placing them at risk of injury, ill-health or, under extreme circumstances, death. Good ergonomic design can help to minimize these barriers and can therefore help to ensure safe and healthy working conditions through the correct use of PPE.

Practices of occupational safety and health can use hazard controls and interventions to mitigate workplace hazards, which pose a threat to the safety and quality of life of workers. The hierarchy of hazard control provides a policy framework which ranks the types of hazard controls in terms of absolute risk reduction. At the top of the hierarchy are elimination and substitution, which remove the hazard entirely or replace the hazard with a safer alternative. If elimination or substitution measures cannot apply, engineering controls and administrative controls, which seek to design safer mechanisms and coach safer human behavior, are implemented. Personal protective equipment ranks last on the hierarchy of controls, as the workers are regularly exposed to the hazard, with a barrier of protection. The hierarchy of controls is important in acknowledging that, while personal protective equipment has tremendous utility, it is not the desired mechanism of control in terms of worker safety.*

-----

28. According to the preceding "Protective Clothing" passage, which of the following statements is not correct?

A. Among the hazards addressed by PPE are chemical hazards.

B. PPE ranks first on the hierarchy of controls.

C. PPE does not eliminate the hazard at the source.

D. Good ergonomic design can help to ensure safe and healthy working conditions.

----

29. According to the preceding "Protective Clothing" passage, PPE includes:

A. Protective gear only

B. Protective clothing only

C. Protective gear and protective clothing.

D. none of the above

----

30. Which of the following statements is not correct?

A. Personal protective equipment ranks last on the hierarchy of controls.

B. PPE is not the desired mechanism of control in terms of worker safety.

C. Any item of PPE imposes a barrier between the wearer/user and creates additional strains on the wearer.

D. Protective equipment may not be worn for job-related occupational safety and health.

----

31. Choose the best answer. PPE may be worn for:

A. occupational safety

B. health purposes

C. sports and other recreational activities

D. All of the above

----

32. Which of the following is not correct?

A. Personal protective equipment has tremendous utility.

B. PPE is the desired mechanism of control in terms of worker safety.

C. "Protective clothing" is applied to traditional categories of clothing.

   D. "Protective gear" applies to items such as pads, guards, shields, or masks, and others.

Question 33

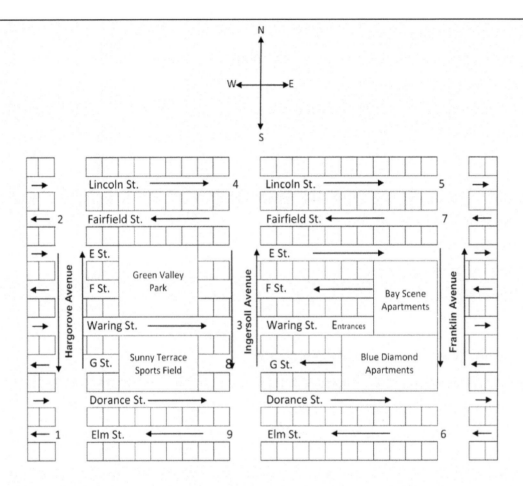

33. Imagine that you are at Dorance Street and Franklin Avenue and then drive North to Fairfield Street, then turn West to Ingersoll Avenue, then travel South to Elm Street, then West to Hargrove Avenue. Near which number location will you be nearest?

A. 6   B. 1   C. 9   D. 8

Question 34

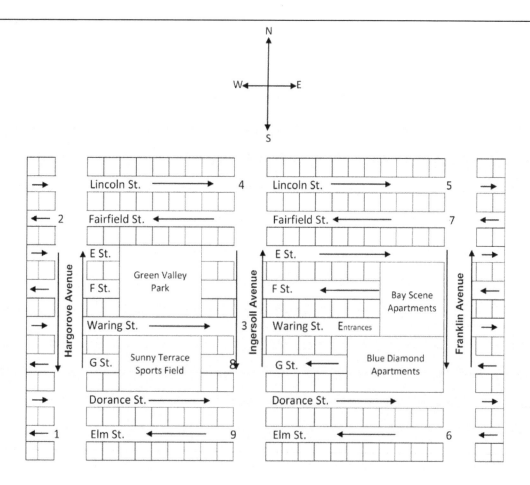

34. If you start your drive at point number 6, then drive North to Fairfield Street, then drive South to Elm St., then West to Ingersoll Avenue, you will be closest to which one of the following point?

A. 6   B. 1   C. 9   D. 8

Question 35

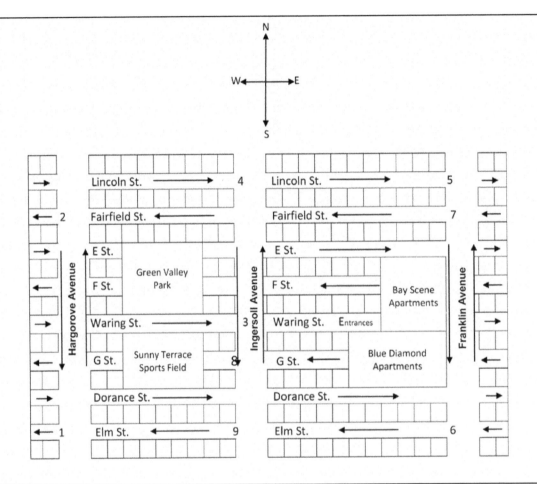

35. You are in your DSNY car at the intersection of Lincoln St. and Franklin Avenue. You are informed that you are needed at the intersection of Elm Street and Ingersoll Avenue. Assuming that you must obey all traffic signs, which one of the following four choices describes the most direct route?

A. Drive South on Franklin Avenue to Elm Street, then drive East on Elm Street to Ingersoll Avenue.

B. Drive North on Franklin Avenue to Elm Street, then drive West on Elm Street to Ingersoll Avenue.

C. Drive East on Franklin Avenue to Elm Street, then drive West on Elm Street to Ingersoll Avenue.

D. Drive South on Franklin Avenue to Elm Street, then drive West on Elm Street to Ingersoll Avenue.

Question 36

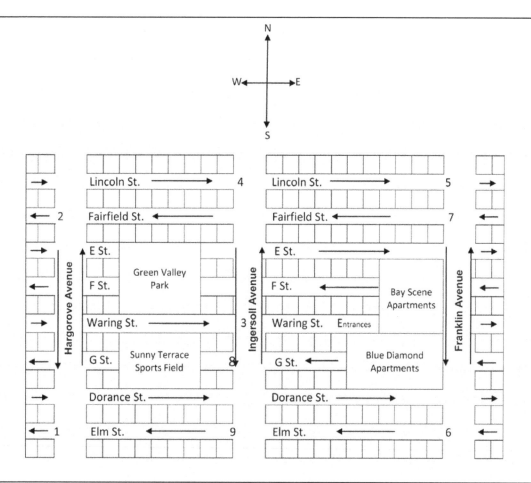

36. You are in your DSNY car at Ingersoll Avenue and E St. You are informed that you are needed at the corner of Lincoln Street and Franklin Avenue. Which one of the following four choices describes the most direct route?

A. Drive South to Lincoln St., then West on Lincoln St. to the corner of Lincoln St. and Franklin Avenue.

B. Drive North to Lincoln St., then West on Lincoln St. to the corner of Lincoln St. and Franklin Avenue.

C. Drive North to Fairfield Street, then East to the corner of Lincoln St. and Franklin Avenue.

D. Drive North to Lincoln St. then right on Lincoln St. to the corner of Lincoln St. and Franklin Avenue.

Spatial Orientation Questions 37 - 42

37. You start your waste collection route by heading northbound on East 64th Street and Wilkins Avenue. After one block you make a right turn and continue driving for another four blocks, at which time you make a left turn. Your supervisor radios and asks in what direction you are heading.

According to the information in the preceding passage, you would be most correct to radio that you are now heading:

A) North
B) South
C) East
D) West

----

38. While in a DSNY snow plow vehicle, you leave the DSNY garage and head southbound. After eight blocks you make a right turn and then after two more blocks you make a left turn.

According to the information in the preceding passage, you would be most correct to radio that you are now heading:

A) North
B) South
C) East
D) West

----

39. Your supervisor has teamed up your street sweeper with another street sweeper to get better results cleaning up after a street parade. You lead and drive westbound. After four blocks you make a right turn and drive for three blocks before making a left turn. The other vehicle loses you temporarily and radios to ask in what direction you are heading.

According to the information in the preceding passage, you would be most correct to radio that you are heading:

A) North
B) South
C) East
D) West

----

40. You drive your DSNY waste collection truck on an unfamiliar route. You drive in a westbound direction. After two blocks before you turn right and then after another block you make another right turn. Your supervisor radios and asks what street you are on. You look and notice that the street signs have broken off.

According to the information in the preceding passage, you would be most correct to radio that you are heading:

A) North

B) South

C) East

D) West

----

41. At the start of your route with your DSNY street sweeper, you first head northbound.

After three blocks, you make a right turn and then after two more blocks you make a left turn.

According to the information in the preceding passage, you would be most correct to radio that you are heading:

A) North

B) South

C) East

D) West

----

42. You start your waste collection route by driving in an eastbound direction. After three blocks, you make a left turn and drive for two more blocks before making a right turn.

According to the information in the preceding passage, you would be most correct to radio that you are now heading:

A) North

B) South

C) East

D) West

Visualization Question 43

Line
of
crates

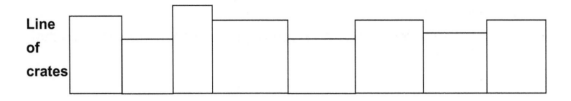

A.

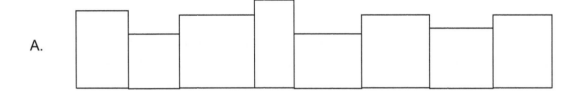

B.

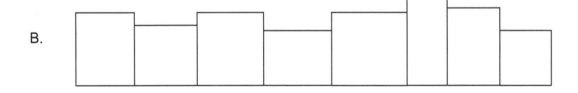

C.

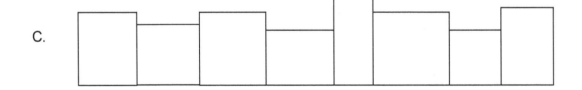

D.

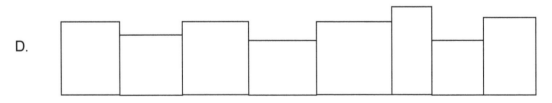

43. The "Line of Crates" when viewed from the back would appear as which of the following choices?

A. Choice A   C. Choice C

B. Choice B   (D) Choice D

Visualization Question 44

Which of the following sets of sections of a rectangle (A, B, C, D) combine to form an exact copy of the "Dissected Rectangle?"

A. Image A   Ⓒ Image C

B. Image B   D. Image D

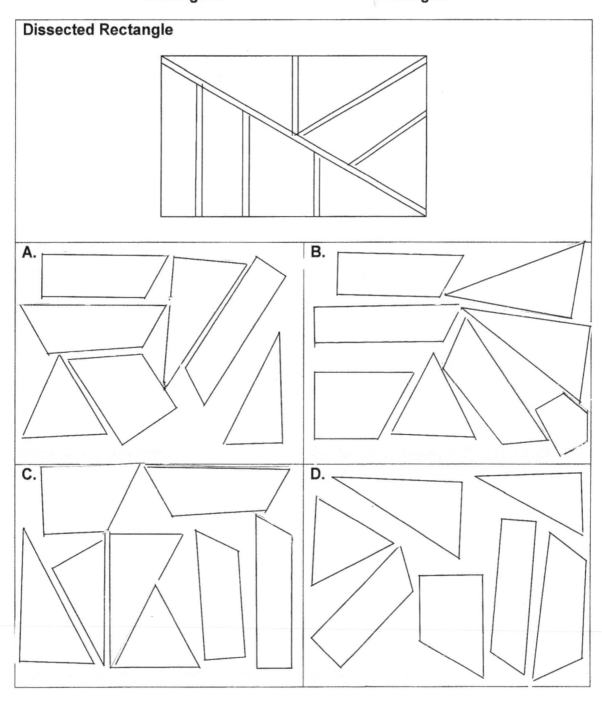

Visualization Question 45

During a special assignment, Sanitation Worker Ben Braverman is involved in an auto accident. He was driving vehicle #2 on Hart Ave. when car #1 hit his car from behind, causing him to hit vehicle number 3.

Assume that all 3 vehicles were in their proper lanes of traffic.

Which of the following 4 diagrams below best matches the statement of the driver, Ben Braverman?

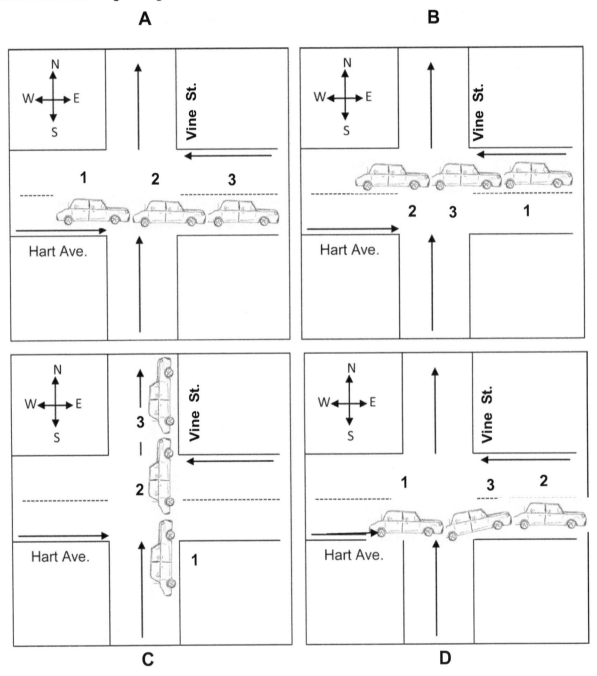

45. The diagram which best matches the description by Sanitation Worker Braverman is:

(A.) diagram "A"

C. diagram "C"

B. diagram "B"

D. diagram "D"

Answer questions 46 – 47 are based on the following accident details.

Sanitation Worker Francis Poller collects the following information at the scene of an auto accident in which he was involved while driving a 2009 Ford Taurus owned by the NYC Dept. of Sanitation.

Date of Accident: November 3, 2019

Time of accident: 7:20 p.m.

Place of accident: Intersection of Chisolm Avenue and Sesale Street, Bronx

Driver: Sanitation Worker Francis Poller. Owner: NYC Dept. of Sanitation

Vehicle: 2009 Ford Taurus

Damage: Vehicle struck a metal covering plate protruding above the surface of the street, causing damage to the front bumper.

-----

46. Sanitation Worker Francis Poller is preparing a report of the accident and has four drafts of the report. He wishes to use the draft that expresses the information most clearly, accurately and completely. Which draft should he choose?

A. On November 3, 2019, at 7:20 p.m., at the intersection of Chisolm Avenue and Sesale Street, Bronx, a 2006 Ford Taurus driven by Sanitation Worker Francis Poller and owned by the NYC Dept. of Sanitation, struck a metal covering plate protruding above the surface of the street, causing damage to the front bumper.

B. On November 3, 2019, at 7:50 p.m., at the intersection of Chisolm Avenue and Sesale Street, Bronx, a 2009 Ford Taurus driven by Sanitation Worker Poller and owned by the NYC Dept. of Sanitation, struck a metal covering plate protruding above the surface of the street, causing damage to the front bumper.

C. On November 3, 2019, at 7:20 p.m., at the intersection of Chisolm Avenue and Sesale Street, Bronx, a 2009 Ford Taurus driven by Sanitation Worker Francis Poller and owned by the NYC Dept. of Sanitation, struck a metal covering plate protruding above the surface of the street, causing damage to the back bumper.

D. On November 3, 2019, at 7:20 p.m., at the intersection of Chisolm Avenue and Sesale Street, Bronx, a 2009 Ford Taurus driven by Sanitation Worker Francis Poller and owned by the NYC Dept. of Sanitation, struck a metal covering plate protruding above the surface of the street, causing damage to the front bumper. .

----

47. Sanitation Worker Francis Poller is comparing the information he recorded in his memo pad (at the scene of the accident) to the information in his report. Which of the following choices (A, B, C or D) has one detail that does not agree with the information in the Sanitation Worker's memo pad?

A. Date of Accident: November 8, 2019

B. Place of accident: Intersection of Chisolm Avenue and Sesale Street, Bronx

C. Driver: Francis Poller: Vehicle: 2009 Ford Taurus

D. Damage: Vehicle struck a metal covering plate protruding above the surface of the street, causing damage to the front bumper. .

Answer questions 48 and 49 based on the following information gathered at a crime scene.

Sanitation Worker Georgette Ruggio discovers that her official NYC Sanitation Department vehicle has been stolen. She gathers the following information:

Suspect: Unidentified

Date of crime: August 20, 2019

Time of crime: between 7:30 p.m. and 11:10 p.m.

Crime: theft of car

Vehicle stolen: 2010 Nissan Centra

Owner: NYC Department of Sanitation

Driver: Sanitation Worker Georgette Ruggio

Place of crime: driveway in front of 34-26 79th Street, Brooklyn

-----

48. Sanitation Worker Georgette Ruggio is preparing a report of the accident and has prepared four drafts of the report. She wishes to use the draft that expresses the information most clearly, accurately and completely. Which of the following drafts should she choose?

A. A car theft of a 2010 Nissan Centra happened at the driveway in front of 34-26 79th Street, Brooklyn, where the NYC Department of Sanitation vehicle was parked. The alleged thief is unidentified, as the theft happened in the evening hours.

B. On August 20, 2019, between 7:30 p.m. and 11:10 p.m., at the driveway in front of 34-26 79th Street, Brooklyn, a 2010 Nissan Centra owned by the NYC Department of Sanitation and driven by Sanitation Worker Georgette Ruggio, was stolen by an unidentified suspect.

C. On August 20, 2019, between 7:30 p.m. and 11:10 p.m., at the driveway in front of 34-26 79th Street, Brooklyn, a 2010 Nissan Centra owned by the NYC Department of Sanitation was stolen by an unidentified suspect.

D. On August 20, 2019, between 7:30 a.m. and 11:10 a.m., at the driveway in front of 34-26 79th Street, Brooklyn, a 2010 Nissan Centra owned by the NYC Department of Sanitation and driven by Georgette Ruggio, was stolen by an unidentified suspect. .

----

49. Sanitation Worker Georgette Ruggio is comparing the information she recorded in her memo pad (at the scene of the crime) to the information in her report. Which of the following choices (A, B, C or D) has one detail that does not agree with the information in the Sanitation Worker's memo pad?

A. Date of crime: August 20, 2019; Time of crime: between 7:30 p.m. and 11:10 p.m.

B. Crime: theft of car; Vehicle stolen: 2010 Nissan Centra

C. Owner of car: NYC Department of Sanitation; Driver: Georgette Ruggio

D. Place of crime: driveway In front of 34-26 97th Street, Brooklyn

Answer question 50 - 51 based on the following "Overtime Requests."

Overtime Requests

1. A request for overtime must be submitted no later than the last day of the month preceding the month during which overtime is requested.

2. A Sanitation Worker requesting overtime must be available to work an additional four hour shift following the end of any regular eight hour shift worked by the Sanitation Worker.

3. Failure to submit a request for overtime as directed in "1" above makes the Sanitation Worker ineligible to work any overtime during the month unless the overtime has been determined to be "mandatory" because of the needs of the NYC Department of Sanitation.

4. The first five hours of overtime shall be compensated at one and one half times the employee's hourly rate.

5. All overtime shall be assigned on a strict seniority basis.

-----

50. Sanitation Worker Vera Checkov wishes to work overtime, but because of personal reasons she is only available to work two hours of overtime per day.
Based on the above "Overtime Requests" which of the following statements is correct?

A. Under the rules, she can work two hours of overtime per day if she files the Overtime Request timely.

B. Because she is requesting less than 4 hours, the overtime does not have to be assigned on a seniority basis.

C. If Sanitation Worker Vera Checkov were to work 4 hours of overtime in one day, she would be paid the same as she gets paid for working 6 hours during her regular shift.

D. Failure to submit a request for overtime as directed in "1" above makes the Sanitation Worker ineligible to work any "mandatory" overtime. .

----

51. Sanitation Worker Vera Chekov works 6 hours of overtime during one week. If she earns $36.00 per hour, which of the following formulas should she use to calculate her total compensation for the 6 overtime hours?

A. $36 X 6 = total compensation for the 6 overtime hours

   36 (6) = total compensation for the 6 overtime hours

C) (36 x 6) X 1.5 = total compensation for the 6 overtime hours

D. none of the above

_____

Questions 52-53

Suspicious packages procedure

1. Put the package on a stable surface or area.

2. After that, do not hold, shake, or carry the package.

3. Do not allow others to get near or examine the package.

4. Warn others that are near of the possible danger of the package.

5. If indoors and if possible, close the ventilation system to reduce chance of air borne contaminants spreading.

6. Wash your hands and face to reduce chances of contaminants spreading to unprotected skin or face.

7. During all of the above steps, remain alert and note any suspicious persons.

Question 52

52. While on your route of household waste collection, you spot a suspicious package leaning on a garbage bag, ready to fall on the hard cement. You gently put the package flat on the cement.

Based on the above procedure, what is the next step that you should take?

A. Wash your hands and face to reduce chances of contaminants spreading to unprotected skin or face.

B. Put the package on a stable surface or area.

C. Warn others that are near of the possible danger of the package.

D. After that, make sure that you nor anyone else holds, shakes, or carries the package.

Question 53

53. Which of the following statements is not a suggested step in all cases in the above serious package procedure?

A. Wash your hands and face to reduce chances of contaminants spreading to unprotected skin or face.

B. Do not allow others to get near or examine the package.

C. Close the ventilation system to reduce chance of air borne contaminants spreading.

D. Warn others that are near of the possible danger of the package.

Question 54

The following four actions (in random order) are suggested when one is exposed to blood or other potential infectious material

1. Isolate contaminated clothes and other items in a leak proof bag.

2. Use an antiseptic cleaner on your skin and wash your hands with warm water and soap.

3. Using gloves, remove your clothing and shoes.

4. Report the exposure and take action to prevent further contamination of yourself and others.

-----

54. Which of the following four choices lists the best sequence of actions when one is exposed to blood or other potential hazardous material?

A. 1, 4, 3, 2

B. 4, 2, 3, 1

C. 1, 3, 4, 2

D. 4, 1, 3, 2

Question 55

Injury or Illness First Aid Procedure

If a person is injured or ill and requires medical attention, examine the victim and determine what you need to do (and in what order) to best assist the person.

The following four required actions are in random order.

1. Keep victim calm and as comfortable as possible.

2. Ask for medical assistance.

3. Keep the victim alive.

4. Ensure that the victim receives needed medical care.

Which of the following four choices contains the most logical order for the above four steps?

A. 4, 3, 1, 2

B. 2, 3, 1, 4

C. 3, 2, 1, 4

D. 2, 1, 3, 2

Questions 56-59

Waste Dumping Procedure

Waste collection trucks must enter the waste dumping station between the bio-hazard and radiation detection sensors. If a truck is determined to carry a bio-hazard or radioactive load, it must proceed to exit ramp 19 and continue to the Emergency Evaluation Building where it will be examined as per DSNY Protocol 839.

If a truck is found not to contain one of the above stated dangerous materials, it is issued Clearance Form 79. It then may return to the waste dumping station where it will continue with the dump authorization procedure. This procedure includes weighing the truck and categorizing its load into one of three categories: 1) organic, 2) mineral, or 3) recyclable. Trucks designated as carrying organic waste must proceed to dumping area 3. Those carrying mineral refuse must proceed to dumping are 9, and those with recyclable materials must proceed to building RB 12. At their designated destination area, each truck will release its load and obtain an LR 62 form which must be delivered to their local sanitation station.

Prior to departing the destination area, each truck must be weighed and found to be less than thirteen tons in weight. Trucks above that weight are required to undergo again the entire waste dumping procedure described above.

56. A clearance Form 79 is issued to:

A. every truck entering through the sensors

B. every load with a recyclable load designation

C. every truck with a bio-hazard load.

D. none of the above

----

57. The dump authorization procedure may categorizes the load of the truck into one of the following categories:

A. bio-hazard

B. radiation

C. organic

D. none of the above

58. If a load of a truck is designated as "organic," the next step for the truck in the above procedure is for the truck to:

A. dump its load in dumping area 1

B. dump its load in dumping area 2.

C. dump its load in dumping area 3.

D. none of the above

----

59. Trucks designated as carrying "recyclable" load 3 must proceed to:

A. area 3.

B. RB 12.

C. area 1.

D. none of the above

Dumping area 9 is used for what type of waste?

A. organic

B. mineral

C. recyclable.

D. bio-hazard

----

60. After releasing its load, what form is obtained?

A. DSNY 839

B. Form 79

C. Form RB 12

D. none of the above

END of Practice Test 2

PRACTICE TEST #2 ANSWERS

Reading Comprehension

Question 1 Answer:

The New York City Department of Sanitation, or DSNY, is the city agency responsible for garbage collection, recycling collection, street cleaning, and snow removal. It employs a uniformed force of unionized sanitation workers (Local 831 USA of the Teamsters) in New York City. Like the rest of New York's uniformed forces, they have a nickname: "New York's Strongest." The section of Worth Street between Centre and Baxter Streets in Manhattan is named "Avenue of the Strongest" in their honor.

The New York City Department of Sanitation is the largest sanitation department in the world, with 7,200 uniformed sanitation workers and supervisors, 2,041 civilian workers, 2,230 collection trucks, 275 specialized collection trucks, 450 street sweepers, 365 salt and sand spreaders, 298 front end loaders, 2,360 support vehicles, and handles over 12,000 tons of residential and institutional refuse and recyclables a day.*

-----

1. Which of the following statements is best supported by the preceding paragraph?

A. All New York City Department of Sanitation (DSNY) employees are members of Local 831 of the Teamsters.
   (**NOT CORRECT**. "It employs a <u>uniformed force</u> of unionized sanitation workers (Local 831 USA of the Teamsters)." There are also civilian workers.

B. The DSNY has 365 salt and sand spreaders and 465 specialized collection trucks.
   (**NOT CORRECT**. "...<u>275 specialized collection trucks</u>...365 salt and sand spreaders.**)**

C. The DSNY does not employ civilian workers.
   (**NOT CORRECT. It <u>does</u> employ civilian workers.** "The New York City Department of Sanitation is the largest sanitation department in the world, with...2,041 **civilian** workers.")

D. Snow removal is a responsibility of the DSNY.
   (**CORRECT. THIS IS THE ANSWER.** "... DSNY, is the city agency responsible for garbage collection, recycling collection, street cleaning, and <u>snow removal</u>.")

Question 2 Answer:

The DSNY was founded in 1881 as the Department of Street Cleaning. One of the Department's first Commissioners, <u>Colonel George E. Waring, Jr.</u>, pioneered such current practices as recycling, street sweeping, and a dedicated uniformed cleaning and collection force.

The New York City Department of Sanitation has its own police force, which is composed of four specialized units: The Uniformed Sanitation Police Force, The Illegal Dumping Task Force, The Permit and Inspection Unit, and The Environmental Police Unit. They are composed of uniformed and <u>undercover officers</u> who handle sanitation related emergency calls, and enforce sanitation related laws in addition to state and city traffic and criminal laws in the 5 boroughs of New York City.

The DSNY police officers are NYS peace officer certified by the NYS Municipal Training Council. Officers <u>may carry a firearm</u>, carry and use handcuffs, <u>make warrantless arrests</u>, issue summonses, and use physical and deadly force. The police force uses marked and unmarked police cars.*

-----

2. According to the preceding passage, which of the following statements is correct?

A. DSNY police officers are not authorized to carry firearms.
   (**NOT CORRECT**. "Officers **may** carry a firearm....")

B. Colonel George C. Harding pioneered such current practices as recycling, street sweeping, and a dedicated uniformed cleaning and collection force.
   (**NOT CORRECT**. "**Colonel George E. Waring, Jr.,** pioneered such current practices as recycling, street sweeping, and a dedicated uniformed cleaning and collection force.")

C. A DSNY police officer can arrest someone without having in his possession a warrant of arrest.
   (**CORRECT. THIS IS THE ANSWER.** "Officers may carry a firearm, carry and use handcuffs, make <u>warrantless</u> arrests....")

D. The DSNY police force is composed of uniformed officers only.
   (**NOT CORRECT**. "They (the police units) are composed of uniformed **and undercover officers**...") .

Questions 3 Answer:

Throughout most of history, the amount of waste generated by humans was insignificant due to low population density and low societal levels of the exploitation of natural resources. Common waste produced <u>during pre-modern times</u> was mainly <u>ashes</u> and human biodegradable waste, and these were released back into the ground locally, with <u>minimum environmental impact</u>. Tools made out of wood or metal were generally <u>reused or passed down</u> through the generations.

However, some civilizations do seem to have been more profligate in their waste output than others. In particular, the <u>Maya of Central America</u> had a fixed monthly ritual in which the people of the village would gather together and <u>burn their rubbish in large dumps</u>.*

-----

3. According to the above selection, which of the following statements is correct?

A. Throughout all of history, all waste has been mainly ashes and human biodegradable waste.

(**NOT CORRECT**. ("Common waste produced **during pre-modern times** was mainly ashes and human biodegradable waste.")

B. Tools made out of wood or metal were generally discarded after use.

(**NOT CORRECT**. "Tools made out of wood or metal were generally **reused or passed down** through the generations.")

C. Ashes released back into the ground locally had a major environmental impact.

(**NOT CORRECT**. "Common waste produced during pre-modern times was mainly ashes and human biodegradable waste, and these were released back into the ground locally, with **minimum** environmental impact.")

D. The Maya of Central America burned their rubbish in large dumps.

(**CORRECT. THIS IS THE ANSWER.** "...the Maya of Central America had a fixed monthly ritual in which the people of the village would gather together and <u>burn their rubbish</u> in large dumps.") .

Question 4 Answer:

Wagons and other means had been used for centuries to haul away solid waste. Trucks were first used for this purpose soon after their invention. The 1920s saw the first open-topped trucks being used, but due to foul odors and waste falling from the back, covered vehicles soon became more common. These covered trucks were first introduced in more densely populated Europe and then in North America, but were soon used worldwide.

The main difficulty was that the waste collectors needed to lift the waste to shoulder height. The first technique developed in the late 20s to solve this problem was to build round compartments with massive corkscrews that would lift the load and bring it away from the rear. A more efficient model was the development of the hopper in 1929. It used a cable system that could pull waste into the truck.*

4. Which of the following titles expresses the main idea of the above passage?

A. The History of Sanitation Workers

(**NOT CORRECT**. The passage deals mainly with wagons and trucks used for waste collection.)

B. The History of Waste Collection Vehicles

(**CORRECT**. The passage explains how waste collection vehicles improved through the years.)

C. The Future of Waste Collection Vehicles

(**NOT CORRECT**. The passage deals mainly with wagons and trucks used for waste collection in <u>past</u> years.)

D. Waste Collection Vehicles of South America

(**NOT CORRECT**. The passage explains how waste collection vehicles improved through the years and around the world.) .

Question 5 Answer:

Waste can be classified in several ways but the following list represents a typical classification:
Biodegradable waste: food and kitchen waste, green waste, paper (can also be recycled)
<u>Recyclable material</u>: paper, <u>glass</u>, bottles, cans, metals, certain plastics, fabrics, clothes, batteries etc.
Inert waste: construction and demolition waste, dirt, rocks, debris
Electrical and electronic waste (WEEE: electrical appliances, TVs, computers, screens, etc.
Composite wastes: waste clothing, Tetra Packs, waste plastics such as toys
Hazardous waste: including most paints, chemicals, light bulbs, fluorescent tubes, spray cans, fertilizer and containers
Toxic waste: including pesticide, herbicides, fungicides
Medical waste.*

5. Which of the following classification of the item stated is not supported by the above waste classification?

A. light bulbs: "Hazardous waste including most paints"

B. pesticide: "Toxic waste"

C. paper: "Biodegradable waste"

D. glass: "Inert waste"

(Choice "D" is not supported because "glass" is categorized incorrectly. The correct category that "glass" belongs to is "Recyclable waste.") .

Question 6 Answer:

Municipal solid waste can be used to generate energy. Several technologies have been developed that make the processing of MSW for energy generation cleaner and more economical than ever before, including landfill gas capture, combustion, pyrolysis, gasification, and plasma arc gasification. While older waste incineration plants emitted high levels of pollutants, recent regulatory changes and new technologies have significantly reduced this concern. United States Environmental Protection Agency (EPA) regulations in 1995 and 2000 under the Clean Air Act have succeeded in reducing emissions of dioxins from waste-to-energy facilities by more than 99 percent below 1990 levels, while mercury emissions have been by over 90 percent. The EPA noted these improvements in 2003, citing waste-to-energy as a power source "with less environmental impact than almost any other source of electricity."*

6. Based on the subject matter of the preceding passage, the most appropriate meaning for "MSW" is:

A. Manually Selected Waste

B. Municipal Solid Waste

   (CORRECT. THIS IS THE ANSWER. The entire passage deals with Municipal Solid

   Waste – the first three words of the passage.)

C. Marked Selected Waste

D. Manifest Solid Waste.

Question 7 Answer:

Waste segregation means dividing waste into dry and wet. Dry waste includes wood and related products, metals and glass. Wet waste, typically refers to organic waste usually generated by eating establishments and are heavy in weight due to dampness. Waste can also be segregated on basis of biodegradable or non-biodegradable waste.*

-----

7. According to the above passage, which of the following statements is correct?

A. An empty aluminum cola can is considered wet waste.

   (**NOT CORRECT**. "**Dry** waste includes wood and related products, **metals** and glass. ")

B. A half-eaten apple is considered non-biodegradable waste.

   (**NOT CORRECT** because an apple is organic and is therefore bio-degradable.)

C. Wood is considered wet waste.

   (**NOT CORRECT**. "Dry waste includes **wood** and related products, metals and glass.")

D. A wooden broom handle is considered dry waste.

   (**"D" IS CORRECT.** "Dry waste includes wood and related products, metals and

   glass.")

Question 8 Answer:

Incineration is a waste treatment process that involves the combustion of organic substances contained in waste materials. Incineration and other high-temperature waste treatment systems are described as "thermal treatment". Incineration of waste materials converts the waste into ash, flue gas, and heat. The ash is mostly formed by the inorganic constituents of the waste, and may take the form of solid lumps or particulates carried by the flue gas. The flue gases must be cleaned of gaseous and particulate pollutants before they are dispersed into the atmosphere. In some cases, the heat generated by incineration can be used to generate electric power.*

8. According to the preceding passage, which of the following statements is correct?

A. Incineration involves the combustion of inorganic substances.

   (**NOT CORRECT**. "Incineration is a waste treatment process that involves the combustion of **organic** substances....")

B. Incineration of waste materials converts the waste into atomic energy.

   (**NOT CORRECT**. Incineration of waste materials converts the waste into **ash, flue gas, and heat**.)

C. Ash is mostly formed by the organic constituents of waste.

   (**NOT CORRECT**. "...ash is mostly formed by the **inorganic** constituents of the waste....")

D. In some cases, electric power can be generated from the heat generated by incineration.

   (**CORRECT. THIS IS THE ANSWER.** "In some cases, the heat generated by incineration can be used to generate electric power.")

————————————

Written Expression Answers 9 - 18

9. A Sanitation Worker is reviewing a report she is preparing. It contains the following two rough drafts. Which of the two sentences are grammatically correct?

   1. Man who commended Sanitation Worker Gail Robertson about thirty years old was wearing a business suit.

   2. The man who commended Sanitation Worker Gail Robertson was about thirty years old and was wearing a business suit.

A. Only sentence 1 is grammatically correct.

   (**WRONG**: Sentence 1 is a run-on sentence.)

B. Only sentence 2 is grammatically correct.

   (**CORRECT. THIS IS THE ANSWER.**)

   Both sentence 1 and 2 are grammatically correct.

(**WRONG**: Sentence 1 is a run-on sentence.)

D. Neither sentence 1 nor sentence 2 is grammatically correct.

(**WRONG**: Sentence 2 is grammatically correct.) .

----

10. A Sanitation Worker is asked by his partner to review a speech that the Sanitation Worker has volunteered to give to a fifth grade class. It contains the following two versions of one part of the speech. Which versions are grammatically correct?

1. Recycling is important it helps the environment it creates job opportunities.

2. Recycling is important because it helps the environment and creates job opportunities.

A. Only sentence 1 is grammatically correct.

(**WRONG**: Sentence 1 is NOT grammatically correct. It is a run-on sentence.)

B. Only sentence 2 is grammatically correct.

(THIS IS THE CORRECT ANSWER.)

C. Both sentence 1 and 2 are grammatically correct.

(**WRONG**: Sentence 1 is NOT grammatically correct. It is a run-on sentence.)

D. Neither sentence 1 nor sentence 2 is grammatically correct.

(**WRONG**: Sentence 2 is grammatically correct.) .

----

11. A Sanitation Worker is preparing a report and has not decided which of two versions of a specific section he wishes to use. Which of the two versions are grammatically correct?

1. The alleged violator and his alleged accomplice have decided not to speak with the Enviromental Control Officer. Both stated that they will not cooperate in any manner.

2. Both the aleged violator and his alleged accomplice stated that they will not cooperate in any way and that they will not speak with the Environmental Control Officer.

A. Only sentence 1 is grammatically correct.

(**WRONG**: "Environmental" is misspelled "En_viro_mental.")

B. Only sentence 2 is grammatically correct.

(**WRONG**: "alleged" is misspelled "aleged.")

C. Both sentence 1 and 2 are grammatically correct.

(**WRONG**: Both have spelling errors, as explained above.)

D. Neither sentence 1 nor sentence 2 is grammatically correct.

(THIS IS THE CORRECT ANSWER because both sentences have spelling errors.) .

12. Sanitation Worker Dino Foster is preparing a speech that he will give at a recruiting session which his supervisor has asked him to attend. Which of the following two versions are grammatically correct?

1. Sanitation Workers exert themselves physically every day they need to eat healthy foods and maintain a healthy life style.

2. Sanitation Workers exert themselves physically every day. They need to eat healthy foods and maintain a healthy life style

A. 1 only is correct.

(**NOT CORRECT** because it is a run-on sentence. A correct version would be, "Sanitation Workers exert themselves physically every day. They need to eat healthy foods and maintain a healthy life style.")

B. 2 only is correct.

(**NOT CORRECT** because there is no period at the end of the second sentence.)

C. Neither 1 nor 2 is correct.

(**THIS IS THE ANSWER. Both sentences are not grammatically correct.**)

D. Both 1 and 2 are correct.

(**NOT CORRECT**. Both sentences are grammatically incorrect.) .

----

13. Sanitation Worker Brenda Rodriguez is preparing an instruction sheet on how to deal with difficult people. Which of the following two sentences are correct?

1. When dealing with difficult people, a Sanitation Worker should keep in mind that patience and tact are both very important.

2. When a Sanitation Worker deals with difficult people, she should keep in mind that patience and tact are both very important.

A. 1 only is correct.

B. 2 only is correct.

C. Neither 1 nor 2 is correct.

D. Both 1 and 2 are correct.

(**"D" is the answer.** Although expressed slightly differently, both sentences are grammatically correct.)

----

14. Sanitation Worker Felix Ming is checking the correctness of sentences in one of his reports. Which of the following two versions are correct?

1. Because Sanitation Workers are uniformed personel, they are required to maintain their uniforms in a clean and acceptable condition.

2. Sanitation Workers are uniformed personnel they are required to maintain their uniforms in a clean and acceptable condition.

A. 1 only is correct.

(**WRONG**. "personnel" is misspelled "personel.")

B. 2 only is correct.

(**WRONG**. The sentence is a run-on sentence. A correct version would be, "Sanitation Workers are uniformed personnel. They are required to maintain their uniforms in a clean and acceptable condition.")

C. Neither 1 nor 2 is correct.

(THIS IS THE ANSWER for the reasons stated above.)

D. Both 1 and 2 are correct.

(**WRONG**. Both are INCORRECT for the reasons stated above.) .

----

15. Sanitation Worker Beverly Ming needs to select the best summary (A, B, C or D) of the following information: (The best summary is the one that expresses the information in the most clear, accurate and complete manner.)

Place of accident: in front of 3645 South 82nd Avenue, Brooklyn

Time of accident: 9:45 P.M.

Date of accident: November 15, 2019

Vehicle involved: 2006 Ford Fusion

Driver: Sanitation Worker Beverly Ming

Owner: NYC Dept. of Sanitation

Damage: cracked front bumper

Details: a private metal garbage dumpster rolled into the street and struck the 2006 Ford Fusion

-----

A. On November 15, 2019, 2019, at **9:45 A.M.**, in front of 3645 South 82nd Avenue, Brooklyn, a private metal garbage dumpster rolled into the street and struck the 2006 Ford Fusion owned by the NYC Dept. of Sanitation and driven by Beverly Ming, resulting in a cracked front bumper.

(**NOT CORRECT**. The time is not correct. Should be 9:45 **P.M.** and not 9:45 **A.M.**)

B. On November 15, 2019, 2019, at 9:45 P.M., in front of 3645 South 82nd Avenue, Brooklyn, a private metal garbage dumpster rolled into the street and struck the **2009 Ford Fusion** owned by the NYC Dept. of Sanitation and driven by Sanitation Worker Beverly Ming, resulting in a cracked front bumper.

(**NOT CORRECT**. The car was a **2006** Ford Fusion and not a **2009** Ford Fusion.)

C. On November 15, 2019, at 9:45 P.M., in front of 3645 South 82nd Avenue, Brooklyn, a metal private garbage dumpster rolled into the street and struck the 2006 Ford Fusion, driven by Sanitation Worker Beverly Ming, resulting in a cracked front bumper.

(**NOT CORRECT**. The owner of the vehicle, the NYC Dept. of Sanitation, has been left out.)

D. **On November 15, 2019, at 9:45 P.M., in front of 3645 South 82nd Avenue, Brooklyn, a private metal garbage dumpster rolled into the street and struck the 2006 Ford Fusion owned by the NYC Dept. of Sanitation and driven by Sanitation Worker Beverly Ming, resulting in a cracked front bumper.**

(**CORRECT. THIS IS THE ANSWER.** It contains all the information and does not have any factual errors.) .

----

16. Sanitation Worker George Vasilios obtains the following information at the scene of a traffic accident:

Date of accident: November 10, 2019
Time of accident: 6:15 P.M.
Place of accident: intersection of 9th Avenue and 64th Street, New York
Vehicles involved: 2008 Chevrolet Malibu and 2006 Nissan Altima (owned by NYC Dept of Sanitation)
Drivers: Harry Belmont (2008 Chevrolet Malibu) and George Vasilios (2006 Nissan Altima)
Damage: dent on front passenger door of 2006 Nissan Altima

Sanitation Worker George Vasilios drafts four versions to express the above information. Which of the following four versions is most clear, accurate and complete?

A. On November 10, 2019, at 6:15 P.M., at the intersection of 9th Avenue and 64th Street, New York, a 2008 Chevrolet Malibu and a 2006 Nissan Altima were involved in a traffic accident. The 2006 Nissan Altima, owned by the NYC Dept. of Sanitation and driven by Sanitation Worker George Vasilios, sustained a dent on the passenger's front door. The 2008 Chevrolet Malibu, **owned** by Harry Belmont, did not sustain any damage.

(**NOT CORRECT**. The 2008 Chevrolet Malibu was **driven** by Harry Belmont and NOT

owned by Harry Belmont.)

B. On November 10, 2019, at 6:15 **A.M.**, at the intersection of 9th Avenue and 64th Street, New York, a 2008 Chevrolet Malibu and a 2006 Nissan Altima were involved in a traffic accident. The 2006 Nissan Altima, owned by the NYC Dept. of Sanitation and driven by Sanitation Worker George Vasilios, sustained a dent on the passenger's front door. The 2008 Chevrolet Malibu, driven by Harry Belmont, did not sustain any damage.
(**NOT CORRECT**. The time is stated as **A.M.**, but should be **P.M.**)

C. On November 10, 2019, at 6:15 P.M., at the intersection of 9th Avenue and 64th Street, New York, a 2008 Chevrolet Malibu and a 2006 Nissan Altima were involved in a traffic accident. The 2006 Nissan Altima, owned by the NYC Dept. of Sanitation and driven by Sanitation Worker George Vasilios, sustained a dent on the passenger's front door. The 2008 Chevrolet Malibu, driven by Harry Belmont, did not sustain any damage.
(**CORRECT. THIS IS THE ANSWER. It contains all the information and does not have any factual errors.**)

D. On November 10, 2019, at 6:15 P.M., at the intersection of 9th Avenue and 64th Street, New York, a 2006 Chevrolet Malibu and a 2008 Nissan Altima were involved in a traffic accident. The 2008 Nissan Altima, owned by the NYC Dept. of Sanitation and driven by Sanitation Worker George Vasilios, sustained a dent on the passenger's front door. The 2006 Chevrolet Malibu, driven by Harry Belmont, did not sustain any damage.
(**NOT CORRECT**. The "2008 Chevrolet Malibu and a 2006 Nissan Altima" are incorrectly stated as "**2006** Chevrolet Malibu and a **2008** Nissan Altima.") .

----

17. Which of the following words is spelled correctly?
A. acceptible
   (**WRONG**. Correct spelling is "acceptable.")
B. colum
   (**WRONG**. Correct spelling is "column.")
C. licence
   (**WRONG**. Correct spelling is "license.")
D. occurrence
   (**THIS IS THE CORRECT SPELLING of "occurrence."**)

----

18. Which of the following four sentences does not have a grammatical error?

A. The personnel department is mailing out the form they want everyone to get it as soon as possible.

(**NOT CORRECT**. This is a run-on sentence.)

B. The Sanitation Supervisor and the Community District Leader has the same goal in mind.

(**NOT CORRECT**. A plural subject "The Sanitation Supervisor and the Community District Leader" requires the plural verb ""have" and not the singular verb "has.")

C. Although he wanted to eat a sugar donut, he decided not to order it.

(**THIS IS THE ANSWER.** It is grammatically correct.)

D. He went to the beach and enjoyed himself their.

(**NOT CORRECT**. "their" should be "there.")

Problem Sensitivity Answers 19 - 25

19. A person (male, white, about five feet nine inches tall and wearing a black T-shirt, dark pants, and an "Atlantic City'" baseball cap) has been seen spraying the initials "SDP" on the sides of waste collection trucks. Your Sanitation Supervisor asks you to be vigilant for a person fitting that description.

According to the information provided by your supervisor, you should: (Choose the best answer.)

A. report to your supervisor all males and females on your route.

(**NOT CORRECT**. Reporting all persons is extreme and not useful.)

B. report to your supervisor all males and females wearing dark pants.

(**NOT CORRECT**. There are many persons with dark pants. Reporting all such persons is extreme and not useful.)

C. report to your supervisor all persons with the height of five feet nine inches.

(**NOT CORRECT**. There are many persons of that approximate height. Reporting such persons is extreme and not useful.)

D. report to your supervisor all males on the street who are wearing an "Atlantic City" baseball cap and are about five feet nine inches tall and are wearing a black T-shirt.

(**CORRECT. THIS IS THE ANSWER.** Persons fitting that description are very few and your supervisor should be notified so that he can take further action.)

20. Sanitation Worker Karen Cohen notices that a fire hydrant has been opened and water is gushing out of it. Sanitation Worker Karen Cohen should:

A. immediately run into a nearby store and see if they have any information regarding the fire hydrant.

(**WRONG**. An investigation at this point is not warranted and does not address the immediate need of stopping the water flow.)

B. take a plastic bag and throw it over the hydrant, as this will limit the amount of gushing water.

(**WRONG.** This would be an unnecessary and probably ineffective solution to stopping the water flow.)

C. warn everyone to stay clear and contact the proper authorities.

(**CORRECT. THIS IS THE ANSWER.** This is not an emergency situation involving major risk to property or people. Alerting the public to stay clear and quickly alerting the proper authorities is sufficient in that it addresses the need to stop the water flow and minimizes the risk of personal injury.)

D. observe the fire hydrant for at least fifteen minutes to see if the flow of water stops by itself before doing anything.

(**WRONG.** Watching the fire hydrant for fifteen minutes is a waste of time and is unnecessary.) .

----

21. During his daily refuse collection shift, Sanitation Worker David Callahan discovers that smoke is coming out of the side of his truck. It has the odor of burning electrical wires.

Based on the preceding information, what is the first step that Sanitation Worker David Callahan should take?

A. Stop by his friend's local gas station and ask him to take a look at the problem.

(**NOT CORRECT.** The truck should be serviced by the NYC Dept. of Sanitation personnel and not by private individuals.)

B. Stop the truck in a safe spot and warn all persons and traffic to keep away from the truck and immediately notify his supervisor.

(**CORRECT. THIS IS THE ANSWER.** Stopping the truck and warning people and traffic to stay away is a good idea as the truck might cause harm. Also, notifying his supervisor immediately will increase the speed of professional mechanics looking at the truck and possibly prevent damage to property and injury to people.)

C. Keep driving as there is a possibility that the problem may resolve itself.

(**WRONG.** Continued driving is careless and may make matters worse and increase the risk to people and property.)

D. Call the manufacturer of the truck and complain.

(**WRONG.** This would not resolve the immediate and possibly dangerous situation. Also, calling the manufacturer is not the responsibility of a Sanitation Worker.) .

----

22. Your supervisor asks you to speak with a Mr. John Forester, residing at 1582 Oak Street (Private House), regarding a complaint that his next door neighbor, residing at 1582 Oak Street (Private House), is continually throwing his garbage on top of Mr. Forester's garbage cans. You immediately notice that your supervisor is providing the same address for both neighbors. What is the first step you should take in this situation?

A. Go to 1582 Oak Street and speak with Mr. Forester regarding his complaint.

(**WRONG**. Because your supervisor provided one address for both neighbors, this address may be the address of the person who is throwing the garbage.)

B. Ask your supervisor for clarification of the addresses.

(**CORRECT. THIS IS THE ANSWER.** Any questions on instructions that are in error or not clear should be asked as soon as possible.)

C. Disregard your supervisor's instructions because they are obviously confused.

(**WRONG**. Instructions should not be disregarded. Any questions should be asked as soon as possible.)

D. Do not ask questions of your supervisor, as he might get upset.

(**WRONG**. Any questions should be asked as soon as possible.) .

----

23. Sanitation Worker Donna Harmon is on duty when a shop owner runs out of his store and says that one of his customers has just collapsed and is unconscious on the floor.

Based on the preceding information, what should Sanitation Worker Harmon do first?

A. Tell the man to return to the store and not create panic in the streets.

(**WRONG**. There is a need for medical assistance to aid the unconscious person. A rebuke of the store owner is unnecessary and not helpful.)

B. Interview all nearby persons to determine if any of them are related to the unconscious person in the store.

(**WRONG**. There is a need for medical assistance to aid the unconscious person. Inquiries as to whether someone is related to the person are at this time not helpful and unnecessary at this time.)

C. Apply first aid and CPR if needed and call for medical assistance and police.

(**CORRECT.** The emergency medical situation must be addressed by requesting proper medical assistance as soon as possible and by applying first aid if required.)

D. Sanitation Worker Harmon should not do anything as she is working on waste collection.

(**WRONG**: Life-saving assistance and calling for medical help is the duty of every person.) .

----

24. Prior to the start of your waste collection tour, your supervisor gives the name and address of an elderly female who complained that her sidewalk has litter that is produced when the Sanitation Workers empty the contents of her waste containers into their waste collection vehicle. He asks that you speak with her so that she can provide more information. From past experiences, you know that this female is prone to making constant unfounded complaints. What is the first step you should take?

A. Carry out the instructions of your supervisor.

> **(CORRECT. THIS IS THE ANSWER.** Regardless of your own personal opinions or knowledge, the instructions of the supervisor must be carried out and the results reported back to the supervisor.)

B. Don't speak with the female, as this would be a waste of time.

> **(NOT CORRECT.** Not speaking with her would mean disregarding the instructions of the supervisor, which must be carried out.)

C. Prepare a report that includes that the woman is prone to making constant complaints and that because of that there was no need to speak with her.

> **(NOT CORRECT.** Not speaking with her would mean disregarding the instructions of the supervisor, which must be carried out. A report prepared without first speaking with her would not be helpful.)

D. Check with her neighbors to see if she has any mental illness.

> **(NOT CORRECT.** The duties of a Sanitation Worker do not involve investigating mental illness. The supervisor's instructions were clear and proper and should be carried out.)

----

25. Your supervisor informs you that you and your partner will have to use Truck #26 for your waste pickup shift. It is the same truck that you turned in the day before because you and your partner caught a bug (on a piece of clear plastic adhesive tape) and turned it in to your supervisor for examination because you thought it was a bed bug. Today your supervisor informs you that the bug has been examined by the DSNY and found to be a common beetle and not a bed bug. As you are driving off, your partner discovers another similar bug and with a piece of clear plastic adhesive tape captures it.

Based on the preceding, what is the best course for you to follow?

A. Turn in the bug to your supervisor and then follow any direction he may gave you.

> **(CORRECT.** A possible problem exists. Your supervisor should be informed so that he may make an appropriate decision.)

B. Stop the truck and go home, as the situation is unhealthy.

> **(NOT CORRECT.** A decision to go home should not be made by you. Also, it is the supervisor and the proper DSNY staff who must decide whether the situation is unhealthy.)

C. Take the bug to your friend who is an exterminator and ask for his opinion.

(**NOT CORRECT**. Whether the bug is a bed bug or not, the proper DSNY staff are responsible for making the determination, and not private exterminators who are not contracted by the DSNY.)

D. Inform your supervisor that both you and your partner will not work today because of the bug infestation.

(**NOT CORRECT**. A decision not to work should not be made by you. Also, it is the supervisor and the proper DSNY staff who must decide whether the situation is unhealthy.)

Deductive Reasoning Answers 26 - 27

Answer question 26 - 28 based on the information provided in the following "Pesticides Regulations."

Pesticides Regulations

Pesticides intended for import into the U.S. require a complete Notice of Arrival (NOA) through U.S. Customs and Border Protection. If this NOA is not complete the product would not make it through customs. The NOA lists the identity of the product, the amount within the package, the date of arrival, and where it can be inspected. There are also other rules listed below:

It must comply with standards set with the U.S. pesticide law.

The pesticide has to be registered with the EPA, except if it's on the exemption list.

It cannot be adulterated or violative.

There must be proper labelling.

The product must have been produced in an EPA registered establishment that files annually.

Pesticides intended for export to other parts of the world do not have a registration requirement under certain conditions. The conditions are as follows:

The foreign purchaser has to submit a statement to the EPA stating it knows the product is not registered and can't be sold on U.S. soil.

The pesticide must contain a label that includes "Not Registered for Use in the United States."

The label requirements must be met, and the label must contain the English language and the language of the receiving country(ies).

The pesticide must comply with all FIFRA establishment registration and reporting requirements.

It must comply with FIFRA record keeping requirements.*

-----

26. Your supervisor hands you an aerosol can to use as a pesticide in your waste collection truck in the event that you notice any rats. The can does not have a label, but your supervisor assures you it has been imported from a reputable Swiss company.

~ording to the preceding passage, which of the following statements is correct?

A. The can does not need a label because it is imported from a reputable Swiss company.
   (**NOT CORRECT**. "Pesticides intended for import into the U.S. require...proper labelling.")

B. If the product did have a label, it must also have been registered with the Swiss Export Department.
   (**NOT CORRECT**. The "Swiss Export Department" is not mentioned in the "Pesticides Regulation.")

C. A pesticide that is manufactured for export to Switzerland must contain a label that includes the wording "Not Registered for Use in the United States."
   (**CORRECT. THIS IS THE ANSWER.** "Pesticides intended for export to other parts of the world... must contain a label that includes "Not Registered for Use in the United States.")

D. Pesticides intended for import into the U.S. do not have to comply with the standards set with the U.S. pesticide law.
   (**NOT CORRECT**. Pesticides intended for import into the U.S. **have to comply** with the standards set with the U.S. pesticide law.)

----

27. According to the preceding passage, which of the following statements is correct?

A. Pesticides imported into the US must have proper labelling, with the following words included: "Not Registered for Use in the United States."
   (**NOT CORRECT**. This requirement applies to pesticides **exported** from the United States.)

B. Pesticides imported into the US must comply with the Geneva Pesticides Minimum Standards Act.
   (**NOT CORRECT**. "Pesticides intended for import into the U.S..must comply with standards set with the U.S. pesticide law.")

C. Pesticides intended for import into the U.S. must have been produced in an EPA registered establishment that files annually.
   (**CORRECT. THIS IS THE ANSWER.** Pesticides intended for import into the U.S..must have been produced in an EPA registered establishment that files annually.")

D. Pesticides intended for import into the U.S. do not require a complete Notice of Arrival (NOA).
   (**NOT CORRECT**. "Pesticides intended for import into the U.S. **require** a complete Notice of Arrival (NOA).")

Deductive Reasoning Answers 28 - 32

Answer question 28 - 32 based on the information provided in the following "Protective Clothing" passage.

Protective Clothing

Personal protective equipment (PPE) refers to protective clothing, helmets, goggles, or other garments or equipment designed to protect the wearer's body from injury. The hazards addressed by protective equipment include physical, electrical, heat, chemicals, biohazards, and airborne particulate matter. Protective equipment may be worn for job-related occupational safety and health purposes, as well as for sports and other recreational activities. "Protective clothing" is applied to traditional categories of clothing, and "protective gear" applies to items such as pads, guards, shields, or masks, and others.

The purpose of personal protective equipment is to reduce employee exposure to hazards when engineering and administrative controls are not feasible or effective to reduce these risks to acceptable levels. PPE is needed when there are hazards present. PPE has the serious limitation that it does not eliminate the hazard at source and may result in employees being exposed to the hazard if the equipment fails.

Any item of PPE imposes a barrier between the wearer/user and the working environment. This can create additional strains on the wearer; impair their ability to carry out their work and create significant levels of discomfort. Any of these can discourage wearers from using PPE correctly, therefore placing them at risk of injury, ill-health or, under extreme circumstances, death. Good ergonomic design can help to minimize these barriers and can therefore help to ensure safe and healthy working conditions through the correct use of PPE.

Practices of occupational safety and health can use hazard controls and interventions to mitigate workplace hazards, which pose a threat to the safety and quality of life of workers. The hierarchy of hazard control provides a policy framework which ranks the types of hazard controls in terms of absolute risk reduction. At the top of the hierarchy are elimination and substitution, which remove the hazard entirely or replace the hazard with a safer alternative. If elimination or substitution measures cannot apply, engineering controls and administrative controls, which seek to design safer mechanisms and coach safer human behavior, are implemented. Personal protective equipment ranks last on the hierarchy of controls, as the workers are regularly exposed to the hazard, with a barrier of protection. The hierarchy of controls is important in acknowledging that, while personal protective equipment has tremendous utility, it is not the desired mechanism of control in terms of worker safety.*

-----

28. According to the preceding "Protective Clothing" passage, which of the following statements is not correct?

A. Among the hazards addressed by PPE are chemical hazards.

B. PPE ranks first on the hierarchy of controls.

  (NOT CORRECT. THIS IS THE ANSWER. "PPE ranks last on the hierarchy of controls.")

C. PPE does not eliminate the hazard at the source.

Good ergonomic design can help to ensure safe and healthy working conditions.

29. According to the preceding "Protective Clothing" passage, PPE includes:

A. Protective gear only

B. Protective clothing only

C. Protective gear and protective clothing.

    (CORRECT. "Personal protective equipment (PPE) refers to protective clothing, helmets, goggles, or other garments or equipment designed to protect the wearer's body from injury.")

D. none of the above

----

30. Which of the following statements is <u>not</u> correct?

A. Personal protective equipment ranks last on the hierarchy of controls.

B. PPE is not the desired mechanism of control in terms of worker safety.

C. Any item of PPE imposes a barrier between the wearer/user and creates additional strains on the wearer.

D. Protective equipment may not be worn for job-related occupational safety and health.

    (THIS STATEMENT IS NOT CORRECT. THEREFORE, IT IS THE ANSWER. "Protective equipment <u>MAY</u> be worn for job-related occupational safety and health.")

----

31. Choose the best answer. PPE may be worn for:

A. occupational safety

B. health purposes

C. sports and other recreational activities

D. all of the above

    ("D" IS THE ANSWER. "Protective equipment may be worn for job-related occupational safety and health purposes, as well as for sports and other recreational activities.")

----

32. Which of the following is not correct?

A. Personal protective equipment has tremendous utility.

B. PPE is the desired mechanism of control in terms of worker safety.

    (THIS STATEMENT IS NOT CORRECT. THEREFORE, IT IS THE ANSWER. "Personal Protective Equipment ranks last on the hierarchy of controls.")

C. "Protective clothing" is applied to traditional categories of clothing.

D. "Protective gear" applies to items such as pads, guards, shields, or masks, and others.

Questions 33 Answer

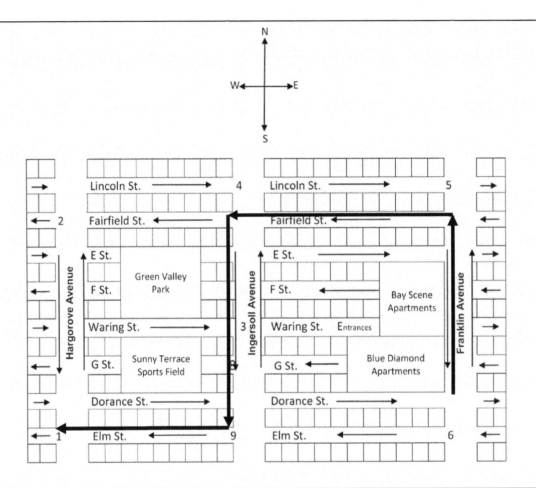

(See dark arrows, above.)

33. Imagine that you are at Dorance Street and Franklin Avenue and then drive North to Fairfield Street, then turn West to Ingersoll Avenue, then travel South to Elm Street, then West to Hargrove Avenue. Near which number location will you be nearest?

A. 6 **B. 1** C. 9 D. 8

Questions 34 Answer

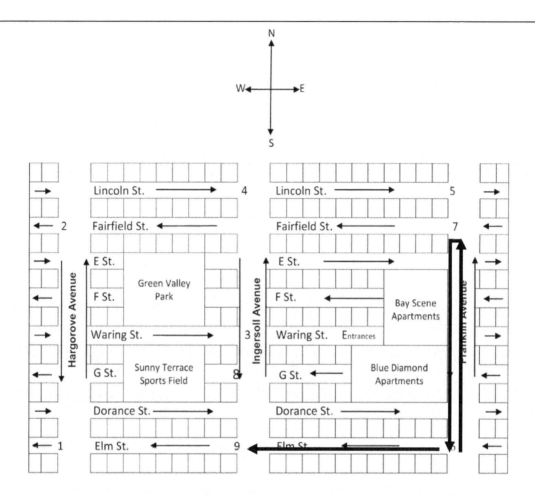

(See dark arrows, above.)

34. If you start your drive at point number 6, then drive North to Fairfield Street, then drive South to Elm St., then West to Ingersoll Avenue, you will be closest to which one of the following point?

A. 6   B. 1   **C. 9**   D. 8

Questions 35 Answer

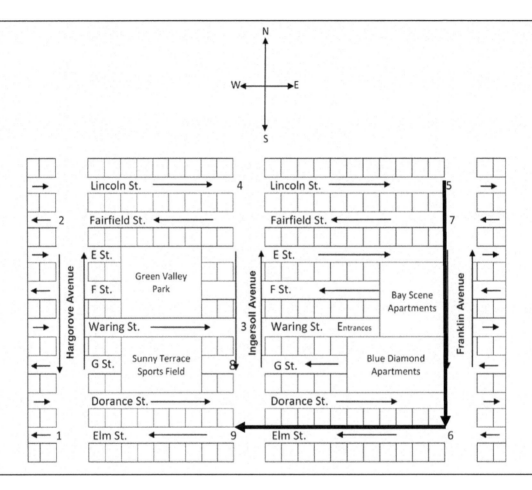

35. You are in your DSNY car at the intersection of Lincoln St. and Franklin Avenue. You are informed that you are needed at the intersection of Elm Street and Ingersoll Avenue. Assuming that you must obey all traffic signs, which one of the following four choices describes the most direct route?

A. Drive South on Franklin Avenue to Elm Street, then drive East on Elm Street to Ingersoll Avenue.

B. Drive North on Franklin Avenue to Elm Street, then drive West on Elm Street to Ingersoll Avenue.

C. Drive East on Franklin Avenue to Elm Street, then drive West on Elm Street to Ingersoll Avenue.

D. Drive South on Franklin Avenue to Elm Street, then drive West on Elm Street to Ingersoll Avenue.

Questions 36 Answer

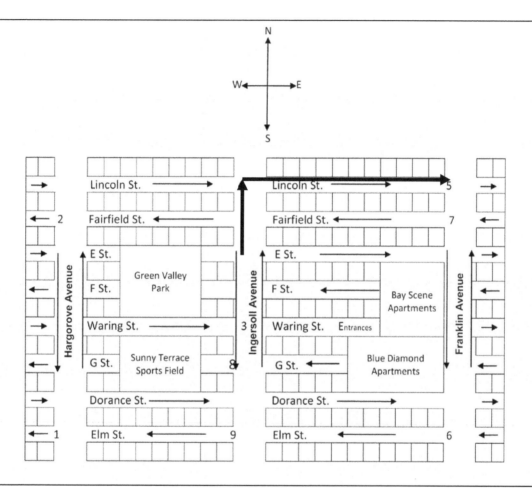

36. You are in your DSNY car at Ingersoll Avenue and E St. You are informed that you are needed at the corner of Lincoln Street and Franklin Avenue. Which one of the following four choices describes the most direct route?

A. Drive South to Lincoln St., then West on Lincoln St. to the corner of Lincoln St. and Franklin Avenue.

B. Drive North to Lincoln St., then West on Lincoln St. to the corner of Lincoln St. and Franklin Avenue.

C. Drive North to Fairfield Street, then East to the corner of Lincoln St. and Franklin Avenue.

D. Drive North to Lincoln St. then right on Lincoln St. to the corner of Lincoln St. and Franklin Avenue.

Spatial Orientation Answers 37 - 42

37. You start your waste collection route by heading northbound on East 64th Street and Wilkins Avenue. After one block you make a right turn and continue driving for another four blocks, at which time you make a left turn. Your supervisor radios and asks in what direction you are heading.

According to the information in the preceding passage, you would be most correct to radio that you are now heading:

A) **North**

B) South

C) East

D) West

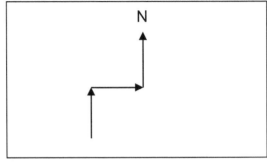

----

38. While in a DSNY snow plow vehicle, you leave the DSNY garage and head southbound. After eight blocks you make a right turn and then after two more blocks you make a left turn.

According to the information in the preceding passage, you would be most correct to radio that you are now heading:

A) North

B) **South**

C) East

D) West

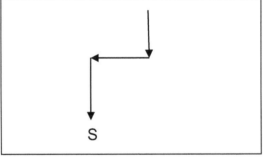

----

39. Your supervisor has teamed up your street sweeper with another street sweeper to get better results cleaning up after a street parade. You lead and drive westbound. After four blocks you make a right turn and drive for three blocks before making a left turn. The other vehicle loses you temporarily and radios to ask in what direction you are heading.

According to the information in the preceding passage, you would be most correct to radio that you are heading:

A) North

B) South

C) East

D) **West**

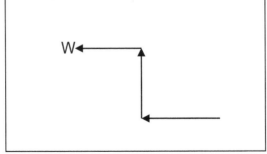

40. You drive your DSNY waste collection truck on an unfamiliar route. You drive in a westbound direction. After two blocks before you turn right and then after another block you make another right turn. Your supervisor radios and asks what street you are on. You look and notice that the street signs have broken off.

According to the information in the preceding passage, you would be most correct to radio that you are heading:

A) North
B) South
C) East
D) West

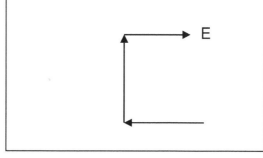

----

41. At the start of your route with your DSNY street sweeper, you first head northbound.

After three blocks, you make a right turn and then after two more blocks you make a left turn.

According to the information in the preceding passage, you would be most correct to radio that you are heading:

A) North
B) South
C) East
D) West

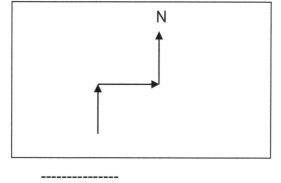

----

42. You start your waste collection route by driving in an eastbound direction. After three blocks, you make a left turn and drive for two more blocks before making a right turn.

According to the information in the preceding passage, you would be most correct to radio that you are now heading:

A) North
B) South
C) East
D) West

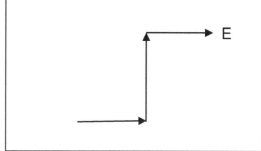

Visualization Answer 43

Line
of
crates

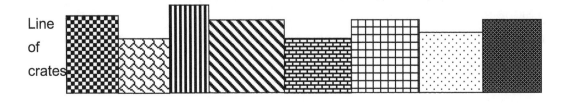

A.

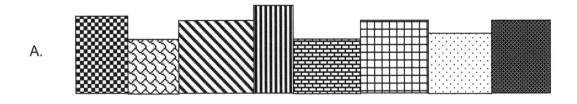

B.

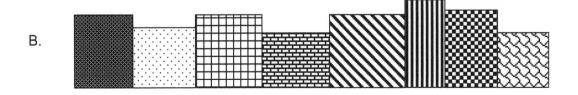

C.

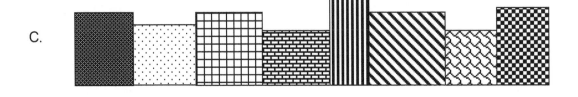

D.

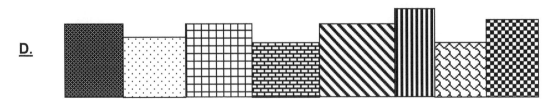

43. The "Line of Crates" when viewed from the back would appear as which of the following choices?

A. Choice A   C. Choice C

B. Choice B   **D. Choice D**

Visualization Question 44

Which of the following sets of sections of a rectangle (A, B, C, D) combine to form an exact copy of the "Dissected Rectangle?"

A. Image A   C. Image C

B. Image B   D. Image D

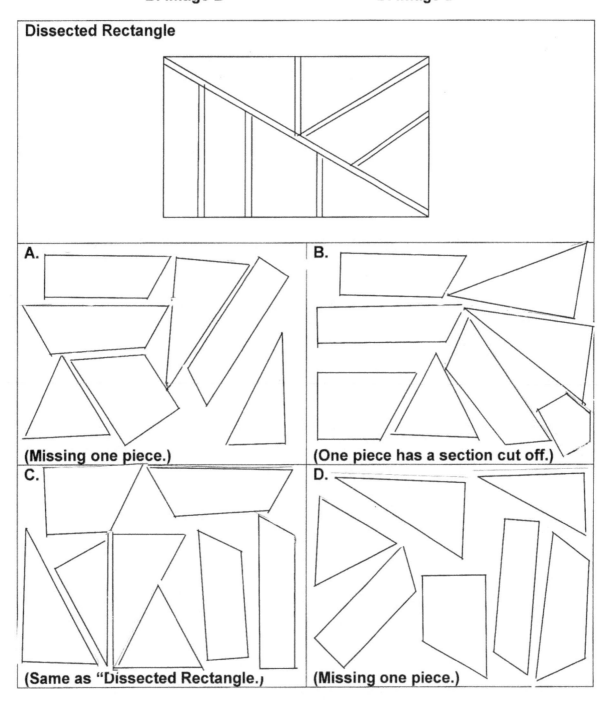

Visualization Answer 45

During a special assignment, Sanitation Worker Ben Braverman is involved in an auto accident. He was driving vehicle #2 on Hart Ave. when car #1 hit his car from behind, causing him to hit vehicle number 3.

Assume that all 3 vehicles were in their proper lanes of traffic.

Which of the following 4 diagrams below best matches the statement of the driver, Ben Braverman?

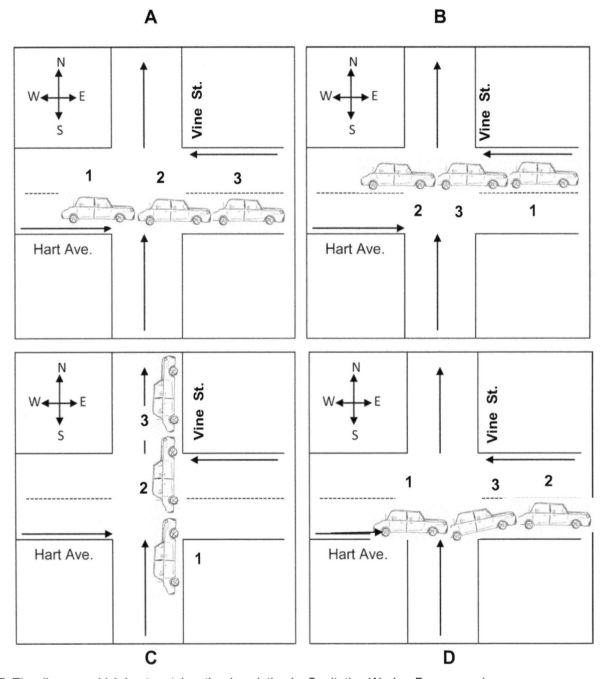

45. The diagram which best matches the description by Sanitation Worker Braverman is:

A. diagram "A"

B. diagram "B"

C. diagram "C"

D. diagram "D"

CORRECT ACCIDENT SEQUENCE IS CAR 1 > CAR 2 > CAR 3 ON HART AVENUE IN PROPER LANE.)

Answer questions 46 – 47 are based on the following accident details.

Sanitation Worker Francis Poller collects the following information at the scene of an auto accident in which he was involved while driving a 2009 Ford Taurus owned by the NYC Dept. of Sanitation.

Date of Accident: November 3, 2019

Time of accident: 7:20 p.m.

Place of accident: Intersection of Chisolm Avenue and Sesale Street, Bronx

Driver: Sanitation Worker Francis Poller. Owner: NYC Dept. of Sanitation

Vehicle: 2009 Ford Taurus

Damage: Vehicle struck a metal covering plate protruding above the surface of the street, causing damage to the front bumper.

-----

46. Sanitation Worker Francis Poller is preparing a report of the accident and has four drafts of the report. He wishes to use the draft that expresses the information most clearly, accurately and completely. Which draft should he choose?

A. On November 3, 2019, at 7:20 p.m., at the intersection of Chisolm Avenue and Sesale Street, Bronx, a **2006** Ford Taurus driven by Sanitation Worker Francis Poller and owned by the NYC Dept. of Sanitation, struck a metal covering plate protruding above the surface of the street, causing damage to the front bumper.

   (**WRONG**. The year of the car is **2009** and NOT **2006**.)

B. On November 3, 2019, at **7:50** p.m., at the intersection of Chisolm Avenue and Sesale Street, Bronx, a 2009 Ford Taurus driven by Sanitation Worker Poller and owned by the NYC Dept. of Sanitation, struck a metal covering plate protruding above the surface of the street, causing damage to the front bumper.

   (**WRONG**. The correct time is 7:**20** p.m. and NOT 7:**50** p.m.)

C. On November 3, 2019, at 7:20 p.m., at the intersection of Chisolm Avenue and Sesale Street, Bronx, a 2009 Ford Taurus driven by Sanitation Worker Francis Poller and owned by the NYC Dept. of Sanitation, struck a metal covering plate protruding above the surface of the street, causing damage to the **back** bumper.

   (**WRONG**. The damage was to the front bumper and not the back bumper.)

D. On November 3, 2019, at 7:20 p.m., at the intersection of Chisolm Avenue and Sesale Street, Bronx, a 2009 Ford Taurus driven by Sanitation Worker Francis Poller and owned by the NYC Dept. of Sanitation, struck a metal covering plate protruding above the surface of the street, causing damage to the front bumper.

   (**"D" IS THE ANSWER.** It is clear and contains all the information and does not have any factual errors.)

47. Sanitation Worker Francis Poller is comparing the information he recorded in his memo pad (at the scene of the accident) to the information in his report.

Which of the following choices (A, B, C or D) has one detail that does not agree with the information in the Sanitation Worker's memo pad?

A. Date of Accident: November 8, 2019

   (The date of the accident is incorrect. Therefore, this is the answer.)

B. Place of accident: Intersection of Chisolm Avenue and Sesale Street, Bronx

C. Driver: Francis Poller: Vehicle: 2009 Ford Taurus

D. Damage: Vehicle struck a metal covering plate protruding above the surface of the street, causing damage to the front bumper.

Answer questions 48 and 49 based on the following information gathered at a crime scene.

Sanitation Worker Georgette Ruggio discovers that her official NYC Sanitation Department vehicle has been stolen. She gathers the following information:

Suspect: Unidentified

Date of crime: August 20, 2019

Time of crime: between 7:30 p.m. and 11:10 p.m.

Crime: theft of car

Vehicle stolen: 2010 Nissan Centra

Owner: NYC Department of Sanitation

Driver: Sanitation Worker Georgette Ruggio

Place of crime: driveway in front of 34-26 79th Street, Brooklyn

-----

48. Sanitation Worker Georgette Ruggio is preparing a report of the accident and has prepared four drafts of the report. She wishes to use the draft that expresses the information most clearly, accurately and completely.

Which of the following drafts should she choose?

A. A car theft of a 2010 Nissan Centra happened at the driveway in front of 34-26 79th Street, Brooklyn, where the NYC Department of Sanitation vehicle was parked. The alleged thief is unidentified, as the theft happened in the evening hours.

   (**WRONG.** The expression is clumsy. Also, the name of the driver is left out.)

B. On August 20, 2019, between 7:30 p.m. and 11:10 p.m., at the driveway in front of 34-26 79th Street, Brooklyn, a 2010 Nissan Centra owned by the NYC Department of Sanitation and driven by Sanitation Worker Georgette Ruggio, was stolen by an unidentified suspect.

(CORRECT. THIS IS THE ANSWER. It contains all the information and does contain any factual errors.)

C. On August 20, 2019, between 7:30 p.m. and 11:10 p.m., at the driveway in front of 34-26 79th Street, Brooklyn, a 2010 Nissan Centra owned by the NYC Department of Sanitation was stolen by an unidentified suspect.

   (**WRONG** because the name of the driver is left out.)

D. On August 20, 2019, between 7:30 **a.m.** and 11:10 **a.m.**, at the driveway in front of 34-26 79th Street, Brooklyn, a 2010 Nissan Centra owned by the NYC Department of Sanitation and driven by Georgette Ruggio, was stolen by an unidentified suspect.

   (**WRONG** because the time is wrong. It should be **p.m.** and not **a.m.**)

----

49. Sanitation Worker Georgette Ruggio is comparing the information she recorded in her memo pad (at the scene of the crime) to the information in her report. Which of the following choices (A, B, C or D) has one detail that does not agree with the information in the Sanitation Worker's memo pad?

A. Date of crime: August 20, 2019; Time of crime: between 7:30 p.m. and 11:10 p.m.

B. Crime: theft of car; Vehicle stolen: 2010 Nissan Centra

C. Owner of car: NYC Department of Sanitation; Driver: Georgette Ruggio

D. Place of crime: driveway in front of 34-26 97th Street, Brooklyn

   (**WRONG. THIS IS THE ANSWER.** The street should be 79th Street and not 97th Street.)

Answer question 50 - 51 based on the following "Overtime Requests."
Overtime Requests

   1. A request for overtime must be submitted no later than the last day of the month preceding the month during which overtime is requested.

   2. A Sanitation Worker requesting overtime must be available to work an additional four hour shift following the end of any regular eight hour shift worked by the Sanitation Worker.

   3. Failure to submit a request for overtime as directed in "1" above makes the Sanitation Worker ineligible to work any overtime during the month unless the overtime has been determined to be "mandatory" because of the needs of the NYC Department of Sanitation.

   4. The first five hours of overtime shall be compensated at one and one half times the employee's hourly rate.

   5. All overtime shall be assigned on a strict seniority basis.

-----

50. Sanitation Worker Vera Checkov wishes to work overtime, but because of personal reasons she is only available to work two hours of overtime per day.

Based on the above "Overtime Requests" which of the following statements is correct?

A. Under the rules, she can work two hours of overtime per day if she files the Overtime Request timely.

(**WRONG**. "A Sanitation Worker requesting overtime must be available to work any additional **four hour shift** following the end of any regular eight hour shift worked by the Sanitation Worker.")

B. Because she is requesting less than 4 hours, the overtime does not have to be assigned on a seniority basis.

(**WRONG**: "All overtime shall be assigned on a strict seniority basis.")

C. If Sanitation Worker Vera Checkov were to work 4 hours of overtime in one day, she would be paid the same as she gets paid for working 6 hours during her regular shift.

(**CORRECT. THIS IS THE ANSWER.** "The first five hours of overtime shall be compensated at one and one half times the employee's hourly rate.")

D. Failure to submit a request for overtime as directed in "1" above makes the Sanitation Worker ineligible to work any "mandatory" overtime.

(**WRONG**. "Failure to submit a request for overtime as directed in "1" above makes the Sanitation Worker ineligible to work any overtime during the month **unless** the overtime has been determined to be "mandatory" because of the needs of the NYC Department of Sanitation.")

----

51. Sanitation Worker Vera Chekov works 6 hours of overtime during one week. If she earns $36.00 per hour, which of the following formulas should she use to calculate her total compensation for the 6 overtime hours?

A. $36 X 6 = total compensation for the 6 overtime hours

B. 36 (6) = total compensation for the 6 overtime hours

C. (36 x 6) X 1.5 = total compensation for the 6 overtime hours

(CORRECT. 36 times 6 = 216. Then 216 X 1.5 = $324.00)

D. none of the above

Questions 52-53

Suspicious packages procedure

1. Put the package on a stable surface or area.

2. After that, do not hold, shake, or carry the package.

3. Do not allow others to get near or examine the package.

4. Warn others that are near of the possible danger of the package.

5. If indoors and if possible, close the ventilation system to reduce chance of air borne contaminants spreading.

6. Wash your hands and face to reduce chances of contaminants spreading to unprotected skin or face.

7. During all of the above steps, remain alert and note any suspicious persons.

Question 52

52. While on your route of household waste collection, you spot a suspicious package leaning on a garbage bag, ready to fall on the hard cement. You gently put the package flat on the cement. Based on the above procedure, what is the next step that you should take?

A. Wash your hands and face to reduce chances of contaminants spreading to unprotected skin or face.

B. Put the package on a stable surface or area.

C. Warn others that are near of the possible danger of the package.

D. After that, make sure that you nor anyone else holds, shakes, or carries the package.

Answer: D. After that, make sure that you nor anyone else holds, shakes, or carries the package.

Question 53

53. Which of the following statements is not a suggested step in all cases in the above serious package procedure?

A. Wash your hands and face to reduce chances of contaminants spreading to unprotected skin or face.

B. Do not allow others to get near or examine the package.

C. Close the ventilation system to reduce chance of air borne contaminants spreading.

D. Warn others that are near of the possible danger of the package.

Answer: C. Close the ventilation system to reduce chance of air borne contaminants spreading. (Should be done "if indoors and if possible.")

Question 54

The following four actions (in random order) are suggested when one is exposed to blood or other potential infectious material

1. Isolate contaminated clothes and other items in a leak proof bag.

2. Use an antiseptic cleaner on your skin and wash your hands with warm water and soap.

3. Using gloves, remove your clothing and shoes.

4. Report the exposure and take action to prevent further contamination of yourself and others.

-----

54. Which of the following four choices lists the best sequence of actions when one is exposed to blood or other potential hazardous material?

A. 1, 4, 3, 2

B. 4, 2, 3, 1

C. 1, 3, 4, 2

D. 4, 1, 3, 2

Answer: B. 4, 2, 3, 1

4. Report the exposure and take action to prevent further contamination of yourself and others.

2. Use an antiseptic cleaner on your skin and wash your hands with warm water and soap.

3. Using gloves, remove your clothing and shoes.

1. Isolate contaminated clothes and other items in a leak proof bag.

Question 55

Injury or Illness First Aid Procedure

If a person is injured or ill and requires medical attention, examine the victim and determine what you need to do (and in what order) to best assist the person.

The following four required actions are in random order.

1. Keep victim calm and as comfortable as possible.

2. Ask for medical assistance.

3. Keep the victim alive.

4. Ensure that the victim receives needed medical care.

55. What of the following four choices contains the most logical order for the above four steps?

A. 4, 3, 1, 2

B. 2, 3, 1, 4

C. 3, 2, 1, 4

D. 2, 1, 3, 2

Answer: C. 3, 2, 1, 4

3. Keep the victim alive.

2. Ask for medical assistance.

1. Keep victim calm and as comfortable as possible.

4. Ensure that the victim receives needed medical care.

Questions 56-59

Waste Dumping Procedure

Waste collection trucks must enter the waste dumping station between the bio-hazard and radiation detection sensors. If a truck is determined to carry a bio-hazard or radioactive load, it must proceed to exit ramp 19 and continue to the Emergency Evaluation Building where it will be examined as per DSNY Protocol 839.

If a truck is found not to contain one of the above stated dangerous materials, it is issued Clearance Form 79. It then may return to the waste dumping station where it will continue with the dump authorization procedure. This procedure includes weighing the truck and categorizing its load into one of three categories: 1) organic, 2) mineral, or 3) recyclable. Trucks designated as carrying organic waste must proceed to dumping area 3. Those carrying mineral refuse must proceed to dumping are 9, and those with recyclable materials must proceed to building RB 12. At their designated destination area, each truck will release its load and obtain an LR 62 form which must be delivered to their local sanitation station.

Prior to departing the destination area, each truck must be weighed and found to be less than thirteen tons in weight. Trucks above that weight are required to undergo again the entire waste dumping procedure described above.

56. A clearance Form 79 is issued to:

A. every truck entering through the sensors

B. every load with a recyclable load designation

C. every truck with a bio-hazard load.

D. none of the above

Answer: D. none of the above (If a truck is found not to contain one of the above stated dangerous materials, it is issued Clearance Form 79.)

----

57. The dump authorization procedure may categorizes the load of the truck into one of the following categories:

A. bio-hazard

B. radiation

C. organic

D. none of the above

Answer: C. organic "This procedure includes weighing the truck and categorizing its load into one of three categories: 1) organic, 2) mineral, or 3) recyclable."

----

58. If a load of a truck is designated as "organic," the next step for the truck in the above procedure is for the truck to:

A. dump its load in dumping area 1

B. dump its load in dumping area 2.

C. dump its load in dumping area 3.

D. none of the above

Answer: C. dump its load in dumping area 3. ("Trucks designated as carrying organic waste must proceed to dumping area 3.")

----

59. Trucks designated as carrying "recyclable" load 3 must proceed to:

A. area 3.

B. RB 12.

C. area 1.

D. none of the above

Answer: B. RB 12. (...those with recyclable materials) must proceed to building RB 12.)

60. Dumping area 9 is used for what type of waste?

A. organic

B. mineral

C. recyclable.

D. bio-hazard

Answer: **B. mineral** ("Those carrying mineral refuse must proceed to dumping are 9.")

END

"Nothing focuses the mind better than the constant sight of a competitor who wants to wipe you off the map."

-Wayne Calloway

Answer Key - Test 2

1. D	21. B	41. A
2. C	22. B	42. C
3. D	23. C	43. D
4. B	24. A	44. C
5. D	25. A	45. A
6. B	26. C	46. D
7. D	27. C	47. A
8. D	28. B	48. B
9. B	29. C	49. D
10. B	30. D	50. C
11. D	31. D	51. C
12. C	32. B	52. D
13. D	33. B	53. C
14. C	34. C	54. B
15. D	35. D	55. C
16. C	36. D	56. D
17. D	37. A	57. C
18. C	38. B	58. C
19. D	39. D	59. B
20. C	40. C	60. B

TEST-TAKING SUGGESTIONS

1. Get a good night's sleep. The night before the exam is not the time to go to a bar or to a sports game. Scientific studies have shown that sleep deprivation dulls the mind.

2. If at all possible, try not to cram. If you can, review the question exercises, practice questions, suggestions, and practice tests. If you have been studying correctly, you owe it to yourself to rest. Cramming often hurts instead of helping. Pace yourself each day and you won't feel the need to sprint at the last moment.

3. Pay careful attention to the time and location of the test site, and wake up early enough so that you will have more than enough time to get there. For more than thirty years I have heard many horror stories of candidates not arriving at the test site on time.

4. At the test site, follow directions carefully and do not take anything for granted. Don't miss any information that might help you get a higher score.

5. Listen carefully to all instructions from the proctor. Familiarize yourself with your surroundings. If there are any problems, bring them to the attention of the proctor as soon as possible.

6. Crystallize in your mind how many questions you have to answer - and also the types of questions.

7. Quickly develop a time budget - and during the exam check the time on your watch to make sure you are not falling behind. Don't spend too much time on any one question (unless you have finished all the other questions and are satisfied with your answers.)

8. If you find during the test that there are questions for which you believe there is more than one valid answer, do not lose time thinking about it. Select the best answer that you can - and go on.

9. Finally - and very important - if you have a chance to double-check your answers, take the opportunity and do so.

GOOD LUCK !!!

CPSIA information can be obtained
at www.ICGtesting.com
Printed in the USA
BVHW062033141221
937BV00013B/492